EVERYDAY RESILIENCE

Helping kids handle friendship drama, academic pressure and the self-doubt of growing up

Copyright © Michelle Mitchell

First published 2019

Copyright remains the property of the author and apart from any fair dealing for the purposes of private study, research, criticism or review, as permitted under the Copyright Act, no part may be reproduced by any process without written permission.

All inquiries should be made to the publishers.

Big Sky Publishing Pty Ltd
PO Box 303, Newport, NSW 2106, Australia
Phone: 1300 364 611
Fax: (61 2) 9918 2396
Email: info@bigskypublishing.com.au
Web: www.bigskypublishing.com.au

Cover design and typesetting: Think Productions
Printed in China by Hang Tai Printing Company Limited.

For Cataloguing-in-Publication entry see National Library of Australia.

Author:	Michelle Mitchell
Title:	Everyday Resilience: Helping kids handle friendship drama, academic pressure and the self-doubt of growing up
ISBN:	9781922265029

EVERYDAY RESILIENCE

Helping kids handle friendship drama, academic pressure and the self-doubt of growing up

BIG SKY PUBLISHING
www.bigskypublishing.com.au

MICHELLE MITCHELL

I regularly remind myself as a parent that I may never get this moment again. Whether my children interrupt me, lie to me, love me, hate me, praise me or reject me: It's always my irreplaceable moment to be the parent.

Endorsements

Parents want their children to grow up to be happy, healthy, strong, kind capable and resilient. To do that our precious children need to learn that life can present challenges and moments of adversity as well as moments of exquisite joy and delight. Resilient children learn how to navigate this unpredictable thing called life through the relationships they have and learning new coping skills. Michelle Mitchell has explored seven things that can definitely help today's parents raise awesome kids in a chaotic, changing world in her warm, insightful passionate way. This is a timely, excellent read for those who live with or work with children.
Maggie Dent – Author, Educator and Resilience Specialist

In 'Everyday Resilience', Michelle Mitchell provides an intelligent, practical and transformative resource for any adult who holds an important space in the life of a child. Michelle describes seven traits associated with resilience, as well as ways to nurture each these traits to fullness. 'Everyday Resilience' is a warm, wise, and powerful discussion of how we, as adults, can build the scaffold to empower the children in our lives to expand into their very important place in the world.
Karen Young - Author, Speaker, Parenting and Child & Adolescent Anxiety Specialist

In our world of constant change, Michelle has identified and described seven key principles that have never changed. This practical resource to help develop resilience in young teens will be invaluable for every parent and teacher today, and also for tomorrow.
Peter Salisbury - Dean of Year 6, Redlands College

I believe 'Everyday Resilience' should be in the hands of every parent, educator, and carer. Offering practical guidance, knowledge and truths, Michelle unpacks seven key traits children need to have in their resilience backpack, that simply make sense. This is one of the most comprehensive books I have read on why resilience is such an important attribute to continually build and support in our young people, yet it is presented in such a highly engaging and practical way.
Sharon Witt - Best-selling Author, Educator and Presenter

Parents need all the help they can get raising happy, healthy, resilient children in a culture that too often knocks the life out of them. This easy-to-read book will help you help your child navigate the travails of life and develop essential life skills and protective traits to aid them into adulthood as confident, self-reliant and empathetic human beings.
Melinda Tankard-reist - Author, Speaker, Co-founder Collective Shout

How our children handle the 'small knocks' is crucial as these will be the foundations for much bigger things.

I would like to dedicate this book to every parent who is taking on the challenge of teaching resilience in their 'micro' family moments.

*Cultivating resilience isn't about
giving children a 'good life' but teaching
them to enjoy the life they have.
I liken it to the ultimate gift described
in the old Chinese Proverb:*

'Give a man a fish and you feed him for a day;
teach a man to fish and you feed him for a lifetime.'

Contents

When Resilience is Shaken 5

The Protective Factor.. 19

Seven Traits of Resilience... 37

    1 Courage 39

    2 Gratitude 63

    3 Empathy 85

    4 Self-Awareness... 109

    5 Responsibility 129

    6 Self-Care 151

    7 Contribution 173

Celebrating Resilience 197

Acknowledgements... 209

About the Author 213

Reference List... 218

Like a muscle that we want to strengthen, resilience will grow with each small choice our children make.

When Resilience is Shaken

Bianca determined that her earliest memories of self-doubt were in Year 4, when her long-term friendship group rejected her over a series of grueling weeks. Dave says that bullying in Year 7 'took him backwards for years,' and he isn't sure if he ever really regained his confidence. Lisa states, 'I would sit in class in Year 5 and wonder what was wrong with me.' Justin explains, 'Things went pear-shaped after I was suspended in Year 8.'

It's a common story. Many children coast through the first eight (or so) years of life, and then identify 'one child' or 'one year' or 'one teacher' that crushed them. Parents often share with me 'the moment' when their child took a hit outside of the protection of their home – a hit from which they didn't recover easily. They seemed to spiral downhill from there, sometimes for months and other times for years. Unfortunately, for a few, the impact lasted a lifetime.

However, many times young ones encounter a string of smaller knocks long before the defining knockout punch arrives. These smaller knocks often come and go reasonably quietly and are, for the most part, dismissed as insignificant. Parents may not notice that they are slowly eroding their children's resilience.

For Jessie, his differences were increasingly showing on the sports field, with his team mates pointing out that he 'kicked like a girl' and 'let the team down'. Shrinking back, he found himself safer in the back of the pack, participating less. He recognised that popularity and playing soccer well went hand in hand, and unfortunately his chances of both were fading. The final blow happened during a Wednesday afternoon sports lesson when he was picked last to join a team. Jessie chose not to play soccer with his mates again.

For Sarah, her learning disabilities were becoming more visible throughout primary school. She was increasingly afraid of participating in class and managed to dodge answering questions that exposed her. She regularly asked herself, 'Why can't I, if everyone else can?' The final blow was when a Year 4 teacher told her she was lazy and didn't work hard enough. Sarah never took much interest in learning again.

Resilience enables our children to be strong and healthy after a difficulty. You may have heard people refer to it as the 'bounce back' factor which allows children to recover from trauma or hardship. Yet, cultivating resilience isn't about what children do in the difficult times. It is about what they do in the micro moments to prepare for difficult times.

The way our children handle 'small knocks' is crucial, as it will be the foundation for much bigger things. It's during the small knocks that young people develop their response patterns to life's future pressures. Parents are wise to see each small knock as a teachable moment that has long-term significance. We can't dismiss or understate our child's daily experiences. They require our full parental attention.

The Importance of Storm-Proofing

The analogy I use to explain resilience in children is found in storm-proofing. I live in Queensland, Australia, where storms can be a scary occurrence. Our part of town is usually safe, as long as you are inside when the storm hits. In saying that, the last storm we had ripped the front gutter and window dressing off my house!

I am personally relieved when storms pass, whereas I am sure that their potential danger only makes them more exciting to my boys. By 'my boys' I mean my two teenagers and husband, whose all-time favourite thing to do is watch a storm rolling in. Thunder, lightning, hail, howling winds – nothing energises them more!

In some parts of our country, storm-proofing your home is essential to ensure you don't lose it. My husband's family live in Bundaberg, Queensland, which was recently hit hard by floods. If homes weren't built or adjusted according to flood-proofing specifications (and some of the old ones weren't), they didn't survive once the winds and rains started. The entire community spent months cleaning up after the flood, but parts of the town that weren't built to handle floods will never be the same.

We can't control the weather, but we *can* prepare for it. Preparing our children for the storms of life, whether big or small, is an essential way to take care of their health and wellbeing. And whilst it has to be acknowledged that there are many things that affect mental health, it is our children's capacity to respond well to adversity that plays a huge role in their mental and emotional stability.

Research suggests that there is an element of resilience that is innate, or genetically inherited. However, research also overwhelmingly emphasises that resilience can be developed or acquired from this innate starting point by exercising resilience traits.

It is never too early or too late to strengthen resilience in a child. Instead of waiting for disaster to hit, we can prepare them so they are better protected in the face of smaller challenges and more able to withstand, manage and recover from disasters.

The Resilience Calculation

Developmental psychologist Emmy Warner explains a child's resilience levels are like a constantly changing calculation: Which side of the equation weighs more – the resilience or the stressors? We have to keep a watchful eye on the resilience levels of our children, recognising that a strong hit at the wrong time – or a string of strong hits – is more challenging for them to recover from.

Hard times can build resilience – or, just as easily, destroy it. It's a fine line. For some children, the stressors can become so intense that resilience is overwhelmed. Most people have a breaking point, so it's unrealistic to believe that resilience will *always* enable a child to bounce back again. As parents we want to do everything in our power to protect our children from reaching this breaking point.

Environments where children have to adapt, learn, grow and dig deep to survive are exceptionally good for developing resilience. We want our children to experience real life pressure but need to protect them from over-exposure during exceptionally challenging times. Exposure to struggles can only develop resilience in our children if they have the skills to cope.

Ideally, we want the challenge of building resilience to be manageable. You would never ask a child to lift 100kg the first time he or she went to the gym. It is not a matter of dropping our kids in the deep end to toughen them up, but a matter of consistently building their capacity and skills. Ideally, resilience is strengthened through small repeated wins, with a few losses in between, rather than a string of losses with an occasional win. This pattern makes learning from life experiences manageable. But life doesn't always play fair.

This appropriate amount of tension can be likened to a rubber band. Pull it tight and it does its job. Pull it too tight and you run the risk of it snapping. The amount of initial resilience children possess will greatly determine their elasticity. When young people are successful it fuels a positive cycle of achievement. When they feel as though they have failed, they don't easily gain the momentum they need to keep trying.

For all of us, resilience isn't a fixed or stagnant position. It needs to be nurtured and protected once gained, and taught and practised when it is absent. Some children experience multiple setbacks at vulnerable points in their lives. It is no wonder that their resilience diminishes. The good news is that because of its fluidity, resilience can always improve. With the right support, children with low resilience levels can go on to flourish in later stages of life, just as much as those who have consistently shown strong resilience levels.

Signs Resilience is Diminishing

Deteriorating resilience is similar to tears in a rubber band's fibre before it hits a breaking point. Parents may describe a list of 'not themselves' signs that indicate a child's usual strength is giving way under the strain. Emily, mother of three, describes her usually resilient 10-year-old son. This description reminds me of the many discussions I have had with families during their child's toughest times. She says that Joe may:

- Break down in tears
- Say, 'I can't do it. I'm not good enough.'
- Compare himself to what other kids look like (e.g. 'he's taller than me')
- Feel that all expectations are too much
- Put unrealistic expectations on himself
- Talk negatively about his body (e.g. 'the girls won't like me because I am puny')
- Get frustrated and annoyed with siblings
- Talk negatively about himself (e.g. thinks he has failed an exam when he hasn't)
- Blame teachers
- Blame me!
- Get anxious to visit new places.

Educators, too, share insights into what it looks like when a child's resilience begins to deteriorate.

When Resilience is Shaken

Stuart Taylor, Head of Secondary School, Genesis Christian College says, 'I see children who are able, begin to retreat. They might hit Year 3, 8 or 9 where there is natural change in what is expected of them. During this time they have to change their study habits, and often have their first taste of failure. At school there is an emphasis on getting things right, but they learn more from failing than playing it safe. I get concerned when kids don't make a distinction between their identity and level of achievement.'

Paul Valese, Principal of Mueller College, says, 'Opting out of activities is a big sign. I'm not just talking about truancy but pulling back from sports, drama, arts, social interactions ... or whatever they used to enjoy doing. Once young people start taking the easier route and pull away from pressure, they start saying, "I can't," instead of "I will try".'

Julie Higgins, Wellbeing Coordinator at St James College, says, 'I know teens are struggling with resilience when they are trying to please people. They become more aware of what is popular than what is right. I see young people follow the crowd once they have suffered a setback and lost their confidence. They are no longer prepared to risk standing out from the pack.

'When you ask young people how they feel when they lack resilience the feedback is strikingly similar. Here are a few statements from 14-year old's I taught this year:

I hate myself and I feel ugly. I am thinking about what people think of me constantly.

I feel stupid and think, 'What's wrong with me?' I don't want to try new things, especially sports in front of people. I am worried about looking stupid.

I feel sad. It's like I am dropping into a dark pit.

I can't go to sleep at night, so I just stay on my phone. I keep comparing myself to other people and I feel trapped in my head.

I just don't want to go to school. I want to sleep.

I eat lots. I just want to make myself feel better. The last thing I want to do is get up and do homework or assignments. Everything feels too hard.

The Storm Within

Parents can't minimise, ignore or even control the possibility of difficulties rocking their children's world. The reality is that storms are going to come; they are a genuine threat. Our children are at risk of losing friendships, invitations to parties, this week's academic award, sporting opportunities or career options. However, there are greater threats to be concerned about. The potential for young people to lose internal traits like courage, hope, gratitude, empathy and responsibility is real. These are the qualities that will enable them to rebuild their losses once the storm has passed.

I would like to suggest that within every storm there are two storms raging simultaneously: the external storm and the internal storm. Our inner state during adversity is the single most important factor in life. It determines how we perceive, manage and respond to the external storms.

I am sure these statistics concern you as much as they concern me:

- 1 in 7 young people (aged 4 to 17 years) experience a mental health condition in any given year. 13.9% met the criteria for a diagnosis of a mental disorder in the last 12 months.
- 60% of children have disorders with a mild impact on functioning; out of those 25% were moderate, and 14.7% were assessed as severe.
- Evidence suggests three in four adult mental health conditions emerge by age 24, and half by age 14.
- Suicide is the biggest killer of young Australians and accounts for the deaths of more young people than car accidents. Three hundred and twenty-four Australians aged 15-24 (10.5 per 100,000) died by suicide in 2012. This compares to 198 (6.4 per 100,000) who died in car accidents (the second highest killer).

In our resource strong world, it is possible to focus on temporarily fixing external storms without stilling the inner ones. For onlooking parents, the temptation will always be to focus solely on the external rather than the internal, as it is more visible and tangible. However, without anchoring the internal storm, we will have little power to manage and respond well to the external one. The storm within should always be our first priority – not our only priority, but our first one.

According to Mission Australia's comprehensive *Youth Survey*, young people's top concerns are depression, coping with stress, body image and school study problems. I find it interesting that depression and stress are amongst the top things young people are concerned about, as they are internal issues rather than external ones. To me, this flags the genuine need to equip young ones to deal with and manage the inner storm. Without the right tools, an inner storm is the most terrifying storm to face.

Our children can 'have it all' (including the latest iPhone, designer clothes and foiled hair) and still be ill-prepared to handle life's storms. It is possible for them to be blessed with so much, but not have the capacity to enjoy it. Despite the posters on our schools' walls and the endless research on this topic, the number of young people who meet the criteria for a probable serious mental illness has risen over the past five years from 18% in 2012 to 22.8% in 2018. For many of our young ones, resilience is much easier to talk about than put into practice.

Helping Young People Make the Connection

Research indicates that resilience helps our children manage stress, feel happier, make better decisions, be curious, cope with difficult situations, learn from mistakes, ask for help, be flexible, enjoy relationships, make the most of opportunities and solve problems. Children want the results that resilience brings. However, they may not always recognise the link between the everyday choices they make and the life they want.

Recently I was in a Year 6 class talking to the students about bullying, a topic the school had identified as important as they had already had one nasty incident to deal with. Students were becoming very conscious of their online reputations and the power they had to gain 'likes' from their peers.

One little girl interrupted my presentation and randomly

blurted out, 'People can commit suicide if they are cyberbullied.' One joy of teaching primary school-aged children is their unpredictable, filterless interactions! This was obviously her summary of a story she had heard. Suicide was a big concept to discuss with 11-year-olds, but there was no going back once the conversation had started. With the teacher's nod of approval, I was now in the hot seat, thinking quickly about how to respond.

'Do you think you would you commit suicide if someone cyberbullied you?' I probed. I'm lucky that she furiously shook her head.

'Do you think it's possible that cyberbullying was only a small part of the reason she committed suicide …?' I questioned.

This started a lengthy discussion about real-life challenges and compound stress, the collection of traits that make up resilience, and how we can use them. We talked about courage, gratitude and self-care, all of which helped me explain a person's capacity to keep going in the face of adversity. Lastly, we talked about triggers of stress (which for these little people included school work, friendship dramas, fights with family, and handling technology), and how our brain responds and rebalances after stressful events.

Although I was expecting this conversation to go for five minutes it lasted over twenty minutes, into their lunch break. Fascinatingly, these students were able to articulate how stress made them feel but were unable to articulate how to combat it. Out of all the questions these little ones wanted to ask me, none was more important than how to handle their internal storms.

Everyday Resilience

Resilience can be a complex concept to explain to children as it is not about doing one thing in response to life's challenges; it's about doing a lot of different things. For this reason, I have found that I talk to children about the traits associated with resilience far more often than the term resilience itself.

In this book I have chosen my favourite seven traits of resilience to expand upon – courage, gratitude, empathy, self-awareness, responsibility, self-care and contribution. These are the traits I have seen protect children time and time again, and have come to deeply believe in. Each one is well represented in research and has stood the test of time.

I know that each one of these traits can have a profound impact on how your child handles life's challenges. I also know that when a child exercises these traits every day, they develop the resilience to draw upon during tough times. Like a muscle that we want to strengthen, resilience will grow with each small choice our children make.

It is incredible to think that our children's brains can be hardwired to respond well under pressure by small everyday decisions. We needn't think of resilience as an exclusive concept that only a few superheros are capable of. It is for all of our children. The micro moments of parenting can accumulatively have a long-term effect on our young ones.

My hope is that this book will inspire and equip you to strengthen the traits of resilience in your child today, and every day.

When Resilience is Shaken

Ideally, resilience is strengthened through small repeated wins, with a few losses in between, rather than a string of losses with an occasional win.

When we don't feel claimed, we feel unprotected and live in a heightened state of insecurity and fear, anticipating the worst.

The Protective Factor

I consider myself to be very fortunate in life. I have two remarkable parents who have endless energy for their children and grandchildren. During a period when my father had spent a great deal of time driving me to airports and helping me transport kids to sport, I had a conversation that I will never forget. I could tell he was tired, and I felt guilty he was picking up so much of my slack.

'Dad, sorry,' I said. 'I bet you and Mum just want some time together. Thank you for getting me through this week.'

Dad replied, 'I never want to take for granted what we have as a family. Family is never a hassle to me. A close family comes at a price. There is a cost involved.'

Firstly, let's take a moment to acknowledge a wonderful father. Secondly, that statement resonated deeply within me.

We need to remind ourselves regularly that parenting well is a costly process. It's easy to rush through life in a blur, not taking adequate time for our most important role. This is often to the detriment of our children who need us to be mindful and present in their everyday lives. There is no way around it; it takes connection, thoughtfulness and time to teach resilience. A close family doesn't just happen – it is *created*.

I can't emphasise enough how much of an impact family has on resilience. Resilience relies on our children being confident enough to adapt quickly and exercise the traits of resilience to navigate life's challenges. This is so much easier done when home is 'backing them up'. The consistency of our love and the rhythms of our family routines all provide a stable platform for them. In fact, a close family, where belonging is freely and consistently offered, is the cornerstone upon which resilience is built.

The Importance of Being Claimed

Researchers have defined 'belonging' as an essential human need that drives us to maintain relationships. Babies do not survive if they do not belong to at least one caring adult. Similarly, young children are totally dependent on us to nurture them. Throughout adolescence and beyond, the need to belong drives us to find our own place in the world where we feel accepted.

Amelia Franck Meyer, in her TEDx Talk 'The Human Need for Belonging', uses the word 'claimed' to describe what children need in order to feel like they belong. I had the privilege of feeling 'claimed' as a child, yet I have worked with countless young people who feel 'unclaimed', and I know the devastating impact that can have on young lives. They neither feel nurtured or protected.

As adults we know that although we have a lot of connections in life, few people 'claim' us. Our social media friends may offer a line of support if we post about ill health, but there may be only a few who phone us to see how we are going, and an even smaller number who visit us. The small number of those who 'claim' us becomes very apparent when we go through difficult times.

The notion of being 'unclaimed' reminds me of the awful practice in my school days whereby sporting captains picked their team members one by one. For the kids who were picked last (and it seemed it was always the same ones) it must have felt as if they were accepted reluctantly – claimed as the last alternative. Or, worse, the last child often didn't get 'officially picked'; they just scurried off in shame to the designated team by default.

When we don't feel claimed, we feel unprotected and live in a heightened state of insecurity and fear, anticipating the worst. We were never meant to defend ourselves in isolation. There is no better description of how children fare without being 'claimed' than this quote from Brene Brown, storyteller and shame researcher: 'In the absence of love and belonging, there is always suffering.' This is why strengthening belonging at home is such an important starting point. A safe place to come home to enables young people to explore other relationships with less fear and more confidence.

One Caring Adult

Many young people face non-ideal situations where family separation (through events like divorce or death) threatens the sense of belonging they should feel in a family unit. In these situations, families have to work harder to keep a sense of security around young people who may feel abandoned or rejected. Single parents distinctly know the challenge of bringing up children on their own, as do families who have moved countries and are not surrounded by extended family. Remember: whatever your family situation is, building a stronger sense of belonging at home is attainable.

For those children without close biological family, the research provides hope. Much research has been done to explore how people who are exposed to high levels of stress still manage to maintain normal function and avoid serious mental illness. According to Dr Ken Ginbury's research, children who have 'made it' despite difficult circumstances were those who had an adult who believed in them unconditionally and had high expectations of them. Dr Ginbury states that, 'Healing is holding every person to a high standard of being their best self.' Love and high standards are powerful forces that can co-exist with great effect in a child's life.

An adult is ideally a parent, but many children have to look outside of their nuclear family to grandparents, teachers, sports coaches or ministers. Even better for building resilience is having a variety of adults to turn to. The more people who have your back, the better. These are the people who will say 'I expect to see the best of you'. As the saying goes, 'It takes a village to raise a child'.

Entry Points for Connection

It has to be noted that without *connection* high standards will fall on deaf ears. As I have said in my previous books, 'Rules without relationship will only breed rebellion.' Parenting out of fear and control, regardless of how well intended, destroys connection. That is why parenting from a mindset of faith, belief and trust in our children is so important. We must realise that *connection* marks the start and finish of everything we are able to transfer to them.

People who belong together choose to spend time together to keep that sense of belonging alive and strong. Creating time to be together is tricky these days, as our fast-paced world doesn't allow for the same type of connection previous generations engaged in. We are often connecting over text or phone while we are on the run. Parents talk to me about how routines like meal times are difficult to maintain, with everyone coming and going.

The foundation for establishing belonging is creating 'entry points' for connection, which is simply doing things with our children that they enjoy. The key is to make sure we are fully present in those moments. I know I am fully present when there is no one in the world who matters except the person I am talking to – when there is no background noise. Screen-free, distraction-free, pressure-free head space results in authentic connection.

Once you find an entry point for connection do it often, so it becomes a ritual for your family. For my family, summer walks have always been a doorway to connection, as have special family dinners that last longer than normal … no phones are present, and we all sit and talk and then clean up together. We practise these routines over and over again. And although the dynamics change as our children grow older, the framework which was built when they were young will always be present.

These families shared their 'entry points' for connection:

We have a family day once a week and do something outside together – a hike, a community event.

We read aloud a shared bedtime story. We also go to the library, which is our thing.

We always eat dinner together as a family on Sundays.

We play a card game every evening and I lie in bed with my children for at least 15 minutes before they go to sleep.

Every February the kids and I take a vacation. We explore different areas of the world and spend the entire week uninterrupted.

I take both kids for a 'family date', and then I take each one individually for a 'mum-date'. My husband likes to play video games with my daughter.

Friday fun day. We all do something really simple like order pizza in and then sit around the table and play cards and board games. Simple, inexpensive and a great way to get everyone involved.

Movie night. Once a month and usually on a Friday. I pull out freshly-washed blankets because they smell good and then we open the windows or put the air conditioning on. We order pizza and buy snacks. Snuggling seems to keep the kids nice and mellow and we just enjoy a peaceful night together.

We meal plan and cook together.

I do pedicures with her.

I always take time off work for birthdays, so we can do something special – just the two of us.

Building Diamond Castles

After presentations, parents often come to me with insights into their current routines. After a seminar I delivered recently, Kirsty told me that each night her son asked her to play Minecraft with him. 'I know in my heart I should stop and play, but there is so much else to do,' she said. 'He wants to build me my very own pink castle, with a diamond minefield. I've been consistently saying 'no'. What was I thinking?! Hell yeah, I need a pink castle!'

What triggered the turnaround in her thinking? That night I spoke about prioritising connection, which becomes the platform for resilience. Kids spell love, acceptance and belonging this way: T.I.M.E. No way around it. 'Will you play with me, Mum?' may as well be asking, 'Do you love me, Mum?' When any parent sees it like this, it helps them reassess their priorities.

Kirsty's son was opening a door of connection and asking his mum to walk through it. Kirsty finally realised that her son was holding this door open! We can hold the door open for our children; sometimes they will walk through it and other times they won't. Some days they will bring little to the connection, and other times they will bring a lot. Sometimes they will bring small things and other times big, intense things! However, one thing I have learnt about connection is that it doesn't just happen. Unless we are investing in it consistently, it won't be there when we need it.

I often get asked how mothers can connect with sons, fathers with daughters, or parents with teenagers who have stopped talking. My answer is to choose something that you both do on a day-to-day basis and simply inject purpose and intent into it. It might be the trip in the car on the way to school, or a movie that you watch together on the weekend. If you have found something that brings you together, do it often, do it every day or every week. Look for doorways of connection and be very careful to listen to any doorways they are asking you to walk through.

Remember too that it is not about the activity; it is about the child. You can be watching a movie together and not be connected. Similarly, you can be watching a movie together and be highly connected because you are bringing *intention to it.* Your child needs to recognise that the activity is secondary to *them*. The conversation surrounding the activity must be the focus.

Finding THAT Group

As children grow, and the relationships they form outside of the home become more important to them, parents often feel a 'pull away'. Many parents feel like their opinion is now redundant, perhaps flat out rejected, especially in the middle school years. At this point the temptation is to 'give them space' when we actually need to be leaning in with an open mind to discover our children in a different season. Finding their place in the world isn't an easy discovery and they need our love and support during the process.

It is normal for pre-teens and teens to take parents on a rollercoaster ride of friendship highs and lows as they search for their place in the world. This journey can be rockier for some children than others. I believe the reason our hearts bleed so much for children who struggle with friendships is that we know how important belonging is *to* them and *for* them. Belonging inside of the home is one thing, but belonging outside of the home is also essential.

I want to acknowledge three big concerns (flat out fears!) that almost all parents have:

- They fear their child's feelings getting hurt.
- They fear their child being excluded.
- They fear their child will miss out on opportunities.

Perhaps these fears drive our children too.

Over the course of my career I have witnessed young people push themselves to extraordinary lengths to fit into a group. I have seen them make decisions concerning drugs, alcohol and sexuality that have damaged their future. I have also seen them 'train till exhaustion' in order to qualify for sports teams. I have seen little children allow others to steal from them just so they have someone to sit with at lunchtime.

My alarm bells ring when young people get fixated on being in a particular friendship group or with a particular friend. I hear statements like, 'I just want to be a part of THAT group' or 'I just want to be friends with THAT person.' Our children have to understand that happiness isn't found in THAT group, it is found in the RIGHT group for them. It's our job to help them develop a radar for what the group should look and feel like.

If our young people understand that they are searching for the benefits of belonging (not a specific person or social status) it may help them make wiser friendship choices and let go of others. Research gives us insights into the three main benefits of belonging, which drive all humans to connect:

- **Acceptance.** If a child is accepted for who they are, without conditions, it provides a powerful sense of security for them. If a child has to change to be accepted into a group, they risk losing their true identity. Relationships which cause you to modify yourself are unsustainable.

- **Validation.** A group has regular opportunities to validate its members. A compliment from someone in the group carries weight. 'Can you help me with this maths assignment? You are better at it than me,' 'Thanks for listening,' or 'Do you want to come out to the movies with me on the weekend?' All such requests and statements validate that we are accepted, gifted, unique and needed.

- **Opportunity to process emotion.** Finding a place to belong also gives children a place to process emotion. When they need to 'talk', the group they are a part of provides them with that opportunity. According to research, people who are needing to process pain often deliberately seek out groups to belong to.

Every child deserves to have close friends who accept them. Those friends can take some searching to find, but we must continue to hunt for them like hidden treasure. When young people find their social tribe, it works. Despite normal ups and downs (unfortunately we can't completely get rid of them!), the positive experiences outweigh the negatives. Until young people experience this, they haven't found friendships that truly work.

Remember that research also suggests that the more teams that children belong to, the stronger the benefits. In other words, the more community we can build around them, the merrier. I see children who are overly selective or cautious lose in the end. Friendship groups, sports groups, interest groups, community groups and neighbourhoods all create a unique sense of belonging. Belonging to numerous groups also ensures that if they are rejected by one group, they have other options to draw from. Encouraging children to be flexible and adventurous in their quest to belong is important.

The Hugging Chair

Some of our children's toughest days in the playground will be when they experience meanness, or as it is termed 'relational aggression'. It's sneaky, manipulative and hard for young ones to describe and know how to handle. Teasing, verbal threats, the silent treatment, sharing secrets, creating rumours, belittling comments, ostracising on the playground or online and recruiting others to join in, are all signs of relational aggression. Hot and cold behaviour that gives children enough hope to stay around and enough hurt to feel rejected are also in this category.

No matter how tough our child's day was we want them to be able to come home to a sense of security and love. While families have lots of different ways of showing their love, Eli shared with me this beautiful idea that I wish every child had access to. She said, 'My family had a hugging chair. If you were feeling miserable you could sit there, and someone would come and give you a hug. You might have to yell to get someone's attention, but someone would eventually come to your aid. Most times it would be a sibling.'

I love, love, *love* the idea of a hugging chair! It gives young people an opportunity to identify their feelings and, in response, pull on those who have claimed them in a very practical and tangible way. I can't think of a better starting point for any child to have in life. It's from the safety of the 'hugging chair' that our children feel strong enough to explore the world around them.

Physical touch, whether that is wrestling on the floor, brushing a child's hair, or taking a moment for a long bear hug, has a powerful place in our homes. Our children feel safest when they are connected to human beings that they trust. They look for reassurance and security through physical contact far more than we realise. Bring warmth into your child's life by touching them every day. If they are in the 'don't touch me phase', just sit close to them and they might remember how much they miss and need it!

Letters of Affirmation

Our words can provide a hug just as much as our arms can. Amy, mother of three, spoke to me about some of her son's struggles throughout high school. These included anxiety, bullying, lack of confidence and, of course, not making sporting teams that he desperately wanted to be part of. This sounded like a normal teenager's life to me. What young people lack is the understanding that life isn't always going to be like this or feel like this. They lack perspective.

As a part of his Year 12 retreat, the school requested that his mum ask people who have been significant in her son's life to write him letters of support, affirming him and showing care for him and his future. They were the ones who 'claimed' him. Amy had 16 people do this. One of his uncles wrote things he would never say to him in person. 'Blokes' don't often get all soft and mushy unless it's a special event.

I know the power of this type of affirmation because our family has used it on birthdays. In years past we have gone around the meal table and asked each person to express their appreciation of the birthday boy or girl. Some years we wrote formal letters and read them in front of invited guests. As our children have gotten older, we have reduced the frequency of this tradition to special birthdays, but it remains important to us.

Last year my father turned 70, and it was a lovely thing to watch all the grandchildren prepare speeches and honour him. My dad has publicly honoured and appreciated my boys on their birthdays since they were little and taught them the value of encouragement and verbally affirming one another.

It is important to create moments where we get to share what we truly think of our loved ones in an 'eventful' way. Let's utilise every moment – including birthdays, at the very least – to speak about their potential and give them perspective.

Funnily enough, my son recently said to me, after asking him to write a letter for his dad for Father's Day, 'Why do you want me to write another letter to Dad? We've already said it all. There's nothing more to say.' Instead of arguing with him I stopped and really thought about what he was saying. Then, I had a light bulb moment! My son was essentially saying that there comes a time when words are embedded in your heart. Words on a page, that become embedded in hearts, are the ultimate.

You May Never Get This Moment Again

Adolescents typically challenge their parents, although many families would tell me that their younger ones are pretty good at it too. I have found that when our children push against our ideals and values, they are also curious as to whether we will still 'claim' them in the same way we did when they were easier to handle. Questions like: Do I belong? Am I safe? Can I do this? Do I matter? Am I enough? are on the forefront of their minds. How we answer these questions matters. Each and every single interaction we have with them is influencing their perception of themselves and their sense of belonging.

During the past 20 years I have worked with a lot of families whose children have been caught sexting. When I ran Youth Excel's Psychology and Counselling Centre, I noticed that most families didn't come in because of the issues they were facing; they came in because of how the issues disrupted their connection. Issues only seem insurmountable when we lose our ability to relate and connect with each other. That loss of connection often started with a loss of empathy.

I remember the day Sue and Graham came to me because their daughter had been caught sexting by the school. They were understandably furious. They literally both left work immediately and booked an emergency appointment with me. Within 20 minutes from their phone call they were in my office.

The school had told them that the photo could never be erased, and it could potentially get into the hands of paedophiles (which was true). There could also be consequences with the school (unfortunately true again). I took a moment to breathe with them both, and then I took my turn to speak.

I said, 'I see this as the greatest opportunity for connecting you may ever have. You may never get a moment quite like this again.'

I could hear the shock in this Sue's voice. At the time she may have preferred that I tell her what a horrible, disappointing child she had produced. But I continued, 'Take a journey with me into her future. Let's look back on this experience. What do you want her to remember?'

When children *belong*, they respond to our expectations far more than when they feel rejected. Authority is an interesting power to have in your hand, especially when your child's self-esteem is vulnerable and at the mercy of it. It is sometimes hard for parents to know how to handle the power in their hands.

When parents contact me during a difficult family moment, they ask me, 'How am I supposed to be feeling?' and then 'What am I supposed to do with how I feel?' When parents call me in turmoil, saying, 'I love her but I hate her right now,' they are really asking, 'How am I supposed to handle my intense feelings?'

Each time we interact with our children – especially during challenging times – is a moment to build a sense of empathy for where they are at. We want to emphasise that they are loved regardless of their behaviour, and *then* call them to better behaviour. It is critical they feel attached to us, not detached from us, at that moment we call them towards their potential.

Some moments in life need an exclamation mark! Our children's big 'stuff-ups' are some of those moments. Think of the last time your son or daughter failed, made a mistake, or did the wrong thing. I want to ask you whether you were able to reassure them that, first and foremost, they *belonged*. And my guess is if you were able to do this, you were able to bring a level of safety and connection into the room that will stay with them forever. (By the way, I am a big believer that children can make a huge number of mistakes even into their twenties and still turn out to be responsible members of society).

I regularly remind myself as a parent that I may never get this moment again. Whether my children interrupt me, lie to me, love me, hate me, praise me or reject me: it's always my irreplaceable moment to *be the parent.*

The foundation for establishing belonging is creating 'entry points' for connection, which is simply doing things with our children that they enjoy.

*We often become stuck due to a lack
of skills to move forward rather than from
the impossibility of moving forward.*

Seven Traits of Resilience

A child's traits distinguish him or her. Over the past 20 years I have noticed that resilient children possess similar distinguishing traits, all which are well researched and have stood the test of time.

These traits have become very dear to me and my work.

In this section I have chosen my favourite seven traits to expand upon – courage, gratitude, empathy, self-awareness, responsibility, self-care and contribution.

I know that each one of these traits can have a profound impact on how your child handles life's challenges.

As you read about each one of these traits, I know you will consider your child's resilience level. You might even consider this a resilience check-up for your entire family!

You may recognise some strong traits and others which need support.

After your initial assessment, I encourage you to use the 'take-home tips' to guide you forward.

Unfortunately, many young people have bought into a fairy-tale that is unrealistic and - unbeknown to them - entitled. However, when young people accept that pain is associated with success, anything is possible.

1
COURAGE
Five More Squats

Bapou: Greek for 'grandfather'. As a child I was awfully uncomfortable with this title. To me, the word Bapou (pronounced Papou) sounded like poo (terribly disrespectful) and rhymed with shampoo (terribly irrelevant). Whenever I called him by this name it was followed by a little nervous giggle. For years I didn't know where to look when I spoke to him!

Bapou was born about 1907 in Cyprus, an island off the mainland of Greece. No one really knows how old he was when he died because he never had a birth certificate.

Like many others after World War 1, Bapou grew up in extreme poverty and left school in his early primary school years to help on the family farm. He always loved books and study, and often lamented having to leave school at such a young age. It was his dream to be educated.

The family of 12 (ten children) lived in a small one-room home, which had an adjoining room for the family donkey. They cooked on an outside stove and had a block of land in the village that made up their family farm. Times were tough and food scarce, so my great-grandparents sent my Bapou and his older brother to Egypt to find work. As the story goes, his parents lied about his age (saying he was 15 when he was only 11) to enable him to travel to Egypt. From Egypt, he then travelled to Australia, which became his home.

Bapou didn't return home to see his family for 25 years. With no internet, phone or money to return to Greece, he was indefinitely separated from his family. He only ever saw his mother again once before she died. His father immigrated to Australia when he was 92, which was a beautiful reunion.

Courage

During his first trip back to Cyprus, Bapou met and married my Yia Yia (grandmother). The couple immediately travelled back to Australia to start a family of their own. During this time Bapou brought his first business, a café of his own.

In Bapou's old age he recalled stories from his early years in Australia, often half in English and half in Greek. I heard about working long hours in cafés, washing dishes for board rather than cash. I heard stories of the cotton field workers living in iron sheds, sleeping on hessian bags, and jumping on the back of cattle or goods trains for transportation. According to legend, there was a period of time Bapou ate wild lemons just to survive. Things were difficult, especially during the Great Depression of the early 1930s.

I imagine there were many times he felt anxious, depressed, and overwhelmed by extreme challenges. However, despite the pain and grief I expect he experienced, he kept going. There is only one trait that can enable you to do that: courage. And he had it in bucket loads. Courage enables you to do things that you are frightened to do. It is the propeller that pushes you forward, in both the easy and difficult times.

People like my grandfather 'smell' of grit. They were a generation who were born into adversity but determined to leave a legacy for the next generation.

Gritty Adventures

I don't want to over romanticise previous generations, as there are people in every generation who are courageous and others who are not. However, I have observed that my grandfather's generation *expected* to struggle in life. They *anticipated* having to push through pain and adversity to overcome before they succeeded. My mother has often said to me, 'Your grandparents knew life wasn't easy and they had to work hard for every cent they earned. No one got a free ride.' This expectation greatly influenced how they perceived stress when it arose. Instead of crumbling, they were anticipating its arrival, poised and waiting to respond.

Young people today often have a very different expectation than previous generations. This may be a generalisation, but I notice that this generation often expect a great life without the struggle. They often don't want to work harder than 'necessary' and feel unrecognised if they aren't picked as a winner before proving their worth. They expect happiness to be effortless. Social media's clever filters convince them that everyone should be good looking, content and wealthy enough to live their dream life.

Perception of how life should play out is something that I believe is affecting our young people greatly. Many young people honestly think they are going to take a few photos of themselves, put them on Instagram, and in six months' time be cruising around on a jet, living a life of luxury. They anticipate walking straight into a six-figure job after finishing university, but when reality hits and they have to start at the bottom, they feel disillusioned and discouraged. I find myself reminding them, 'If you want to have a great life, expect it to cost you something. Expect life to be a gritty adventure, rather than a walk in the park.'

We can be doing our children a great disservice by only providing them with examples of wealth and happiness.

Experiences outside of the home can broaden young people's perspective and give them a more realistic understanding of the world. A volunteering position or trip to a third-world country may be exactly what they need.

In real life, no one is 'up' all the time. No one wins all the time. Real life is a rollercoaster of highs and lows, wins and losses, and so much in between that you can't control. Hard work is the route to long-term success, and there are no overnight wonders. Unfortunately, many young people have bought into a fairy-tale that is unrealistic and – unbeknown to them – entitled. However, when young people accept that pain is associated with success, anything is possible.

Living Openly

We don't always need to expose our children to the big hardships or stresses we experience as adults. However, our children need to see an appropriate range of emotions as we handle everyday anxieties. When we live openly, honestly and transparently, our children see us in every season. The glory of parenting (and grandparenting) is to be an example through life's challenges. When young people don't get this example, they develop superficial understandings of what constitute success.

It's not good for our children to believe that adults *always* have it 'together'. That is why I believe that we need to engage in more transparent dialogue about pain. Where it might be functional to deny feelings in the moment, we need to help our children understand that pain is an important motivator to teach us. When we don't talk about pain, we put our children under pressure to 'suck it up' – as it may appear that we do. Children need to see that courage is not invulnerability. It is not being 'tough'. People can feel deeply and still come out fighting.

When I asked a group of students how their parents hid anxiety or pain, I found some insightful responses:

Chloe, 14, says, 'I have never seen my dad angry or upset. I thought he was invincible until he and Mum got a divorce. Then I felt like I didn't know who he really was.'

Sam, 15, says, 'Mum never asks for help. I don't think it's good that she does everything herself.'

Sarah, 17, says, 'There is no class in school that tells you what to do when you are feeling down. I never knew how to handle it because my parents never appeared to have any issues. I thought I was the only one. I wish they had at least talked to me about times they were depressed.'

One of the best things our children can see us do is ask for help. Brene Brown, storyteller and shame researcher, says, 'There are only two children in the world: those who ask for help and those who don't.' Our children will pay a major price if they don't learn to process pain well or aren't prepared to ask for help to find out how.

Our children need to fully experience their feelings before they can respond appropriately to them. Those who achieve amazing things embrace fear without being afraid of the fear itself. They feel the pain, but they move forward in spite of it. We do our children a great disservice when we over-protect them from experiencing negative emotions. Instead, we need to help our children become familiar with pain, fear, anger and sadness. My advice is to lean into strong emotion rather than away from it. This is the quickest way to help children navigate their way through it.

My Concern with Today's Language

The reality is that each person's mental health is continually in a state of flux.

Feeling sad or anxious is actually a normal part of being a human being. Becoming stuck in a place of depression or anxiety or wildly fluctuating emotions isn't a healthy place to live. We often become stuck due to a lack of skills to move forward rather than from the impossibility of moving forward.

I get concerned about young people being partially educated when it comes to their mental health. They know enough to throw terms like 'depression' around and are comfortable diagnosing each other using checklists on the internet. What they aren't as good at is knowing how to combat those feelings. It is critical that we focus on educating young people about skills they need to remain strong.

I notice that when young people feel stressed it's easy for them to opt out by saying they feel depressed or anxious. It's not so much an excuse but a mindset that says, 'When I experience negative feelings, I stop playing the game'. I have seen many young people drop out of school, isolate themselves from peers or escape to the online world because they didn't believe they had the strength to continue. Many young people's addiction to gaming started out as a desire to escape. The online world became their 'go to' every time they didn't want to engage in real-life problem solving.

Many young people experience strong emotion in response to life's challenges. However, anxiety or depression don't have to be a lifelong diagnosis if young people are prepared to keep walking forward. The big question is: how do we teach our children to keep making decisions, taking risks and solving problems, even in the face of negative feelings?

Resistance Training

The best way I can help parents understand the role they play in developing resilience is by using the following analogy: Think of a young person's life like a big gym session (with lots of squats), and a parent like a personal trainer. Just like a personal trainer, a parent needs to help their child develop a tolerance for 'the burn' that comes from doing life's squats. They must help them develop capacity to grow, fail, get up again, fail some more … and conquer their dreams. Our children need to know how to respond when they meet resistance.

We don't want our children to push past their emotional capacity to the point of burnout, but we *do* want them to know how to work with the burn and get another five squats out of themselves. In other words: don't squat them to death, but stretch their capacity.

Our job as parent coach is critical. A poor coach would allow them to sit the session out every time they experience 'the burn'. He or she would pull up a chair, bring them a can of Coke and say, 'Take a rest. Sit this one out. I know we are supposed to be training today, but you look tired. There is always tomorrow.'

A great coach will probably do the opposite. He or she might say, 'You can do it. You've got five more squats in you. Stay focused. Let me wipe your sweat. Let me count you down. If you need to shake it out, that's okay. If you need to breathe then breathe, but stay on course.'

There is a real art to saying, 'I believe you can' creatively. The idea is to acknowledge pain while reminding young people of their strengths, abilities, relationships and innate worth. Words like, 'You have no reason to be so hard on yourself,' 'You were made for this,' or 'This will be a lot easier than you think' reassure children. A gentle push forward is, at times, important. The fertiliser for courage is *encouragement*. When the right word is spoken at the right time, it goes deep into our children's heart and accelerates courage.

Courage to Raise Your Hand

It's often the new, little experiences involved with growing up that cause our children stress. Patiently encouraging our children to 'have a go at', firstly with us and then autonomously, can help them move past these initial fears. We have to remember that our children are changing at lightning speed, and so much in their world is new. It's therefore understandable they may need repeat exposure to new things, and time to build resilience to them.

Here are some statements from parents that you might relate to:

My child doesn't want to be left at dance class on her own. We have to work really hard at getting her to stay there by herself. Trying anything on her own is actually a big effort.

My son refuses to pay for groceries or go into the shops on his own. He doesn't want to look silly and he won't let me teach him how to use an ATM card.

My son has a meltdown about wearing a collared shirt or getting dressed up to go out. I think it is the fact that he feels different than he usually does.

My daughter just refuses to carry a present into a birthday party. I can't quite work out why she feels so uncomfortable about it. I would feel more uncomfortable about not having a present to bring!

My daughter has never been a confident reader. Getting her to read aloud is a major effort.

A few of my daughter's friends shave their legs and now she is really self-conscious on swimming days. She doesn't even have a lot of hairs on her legs, but she feels different.

I notice that my son won't try anything that he feels his friends won't approve of. He doesn't want to get laughed at so he plays it safe.

Asking for help when we feel scared or unsure is something that our children should learn as early as possible. I recently spoke to

Courage

a group of Year 5 students about anxiety and asked them if they ever feel uncomfortable asking for help with their school work or putting up their hand in class. All the children related to that feeling, except a few clever individuals who put up their hand to tell me so (haha).

Although students may know on a logical level that they are at school to learn, and asking questions is showing good learning skills, it still challenges them. Asking for help singles them out and makes them feel vulnerable to someone's judgement and response. Some fear being laughed at by peers, which is enough to deter them. As Tahlia put it, 'I feel insecure and very self-conscious about asking questions. It's like everyone is looking at me saying, "What is she doing in this class if she isn't smart enough to be here?"'

When I was a teacher I used to have a segment every day called 'There are No Stupid Questions,' where I encouraged students to ask a question about anything they didn't understand during that day. My Year 4 class loved it! My aim was to get children practising asking questions in a safe environment where they knew they would be praised and rewarded with lollies or stickers for being inquisitive. Once young people realised asking questions could be a positive experience, they were less likely to fear it.

Finding ways to deliberately create space for our children to ask questions at home isn't as hard as it sounds. If we don't create space for it, it may not happen. Here are some thoughts to help:

- Do homework during a time when parents are available to answer questions. If we are not accessible, our children may not seek us out.

- Use travel time to take turns to ask each other questions. This ensures the car ride home in the afternoon is not just a one-way conversation.

- Create one-on-one time with each of your children. This provides them with the privacy to ask you sensitive questions.

- Recognise the importance of a bedtime routine. This provides children with a regular opportunity to ask you questions.

- If a child is brave enough to bring up a topic like pornography or sex, please have the utmost respect for the courage that it may have taken. Give your response the time and attention it deserves.

- Don't interfere with their conversations by answering for them or asking questions on their behalf. Let them speak for themselves, and then reflect with them at a later stage.

- Always be attentive to the first question children ask! Our children often 'test the waters' by asking a non-threatening question before asking more intense questions.

Push Back with Truth

My mother-in-law says: 'Seventy percent of people are kind, seventy percent of the time.' With this in mind we need to help our children know when to speak up and when to be gracious and accept the reality of human nature! I often say to young people: if someone is mean once, you are best to write it off as a bad day. If someone is mean to you twice, you might overlook it. But if someone is mean to you consistently, you are going to need a strategy.

Courage

It is tempting to try and combat meanness with meanness. Name calling, threatening, spreading rumours and rounding up other friends for support are all desperate moves that seldom work. Mean words + mean words usually turn a bad day into a disaster.

That is why I like to teach young people that the most effective (and courageous) way to handle meanness is by 'pushing back' with truth. The good news is that you can teach this strategy to children at home.

Kylie asked me how she could help her six-year-old, who was consistently being called 'fat' at school. Her usually happy daughter, was becoming anxious and clingy. She had even asked her mother to take her to the doctors to help her lose weight (at six!). This little girl needed strategies to cope, quickly.

I asked her mother to start practising short, sharp, snappy statements with her, so she knew exactly what to do and say when she was at school. These statements needed to be grounded in truth rather than meanness. They were comeback lines such as, 'Stop. No. I'm NOT fat!" "Excuse me!" or 'I don't think you should be saying that, do you?'

The words also needed to be accompanied by strong body language that emphasised that she meant what she said. We often forget that communication is 70% body language. Practice was the key, as she wasn't accustomed to having to be so forthright. She preferred to be softer, but sometimes strong words are important.

It takes a lot of courage to 'push back' with truth, but when children are able to, it often stops meanness in its tracks. Here are some examples which show the difference between pushing back with truth and pushing back with meanness:

Mean statement: You're an idiot.
Pushing back with meanness – You're an idiot too.
Pushing back with truth – No I'm not!

Mean statement: I'm not your friend anymore.
Pushing back with meanness – Fine. I never want to talk to you again.
Pushing back with truth – That's okay. I've got other friends.

Mean statement: You suck.
Pushing back with meanness – Who are you to talk? Do you know how annoying you are! You suck double.
Pushing back with truth – That's not very nice!

Now, here's an important PS. Sometimes children choose to be mean because they know they'll get a reaction. In this situation, children are better off talking to the person being mean when no one else is around. A private one-on-one conversation, with or without an adult's help, can work better. Remember, children don't always have to push back with truth in front of a big crowd of people. Sometimes it is best to tell a person how you feel without an audience.

When That Doesn't Work

Rob, 12 turning 13, was getting teased for having red hair by two boys who were a few years older than him. Every lunchtime they found him to taunt him, and often 'warmed their hands' over his

Courage

head. Needless to say, this lad was intimidated and humiliated. What could he do?

Unfortunately, there is no one fool proof strategy that is a teenager's golden ticket to freedom from meanness. If Rob were in primary school, I would encourage him to use short, sharp snappy statements. While this may still work, high school brings a lot more variables with it, so the outcome is far more unpredictable. He needed to have a few more tricks up his sleeve. Rob could also try:

- Using humour to diffuse things, especially if there's some truth in what is being said. Try saying, 'Come on boys! You're just jealous,' followed by a laugh. When you genuinely laugh during a tense situation it tends to diffuse things.

- Agreeing with the person being mean. For example, 'Yep, red hair is a bit different.' A limited reaction might make them lose interest.

- Ignoring the person being mean. Just look straight through them and walk away.

- Travelling in packs whenever possible or staying near places which are well supervised, like libraries and ovals. That will give children the best shot at being protected, and someone else might see and report what's happening.

- Learning self-defence might be helpful. The mind, body connection is a lot more powerful that many of us realise. Just knowing how to defend yourself can make children feel more confident.

- Keeping a daily journal of what's happening. This can help children report meanness with facts rather than just emotional stories. Write down what the other person (or people) said or did, as well as where it happened, when it happened, and if it's happening to anyone else.

- Remember, talking to a helpful adult is only a decision away. Children don't have to put up with someone being consistently mean. It's not okay. Although telling a teacher or adult is the ideal, research says that most young people don't because they fear the backlash. As adults we need to be mindful of this.

Young people often tell me that they want to help when someone is being 'picked on' but don't always know what to do. Perhaps instead of directly standing up to the bully, they are better off supporting the victim. I suggest children make their presence known by making eye contact, smiling or standing close to the victim. This type of support actually strengthens and empowers the victim without creating more conflict.

Courage to Stand Alone

Maria, a mum, talked to me about her daughter's friendship problems. It sounded as if her daughter was on the bottom of the pecking order amongst a group of highly competitive girls. She was consistently excluded from conversations and parties, and regularly in tears at home. Things climaxed after they 'Facetimed her' from a party that she wasn't invited to.

Her daughter had to decide whether to stay in the group or leave to find friends who would embrace her more willingly.

Understandably, she was hesitant to leave her friendship group because she feared the unknown. Would she be accepted elsewhere, or would she be permanently left by herself at lunchtime? This decision required enormous amounts of courage.

I was so impressed by how her parents handled the situation. They consistently reinforced that standing alone was a legitimate option. Her mother explained, 'We tell our girls that their own company is okay. If they have to 'lone it' at lunchtime, that's fine. My eldest would sometimes go to the library by herself if that was what she needed to do. She knows she will always come home to her family who love her. If our children have had a bad day, we tell them stories about when that happened to us at school. That way they know what they are going through happens to everyone.'

There have been many men and women from history who consciously chose to 'stand alone'. They defended deep convictions, beliefs, ideas and dreams. They also chose to stand alone to protect other people. In some ways it is the most powerful place to stand. It is far better to be alone than compromise who you are. But embracing loneliness takes courage, especially for a young person.

When you ask students to recall a time when they stood alone, they are quick to share their experiences. Young people might stand alone when someone misunderstands them, judges them, rejects them or their ideas, or wants them to do something they are uncomfortable with. Surprisingly, standing alone is often admired by peers, and being true to yourself is usually the best response to being rejected by others.

Standing alone is like treading water. It's not ideal in the long term, but in the short term it can be a life saver. It takes some young people longer than others to find a group they belong to. In the meantime, their sense of belonging to themselves and belonging at home is critical. Young people are far better off being on their own than compromising who they are.

This is one of life's big and brutal concepts: people might choose not to like us. OUCH! And yes, this genuinely hurts. It's also possible that people might like us for a while and then change their mind. In other words, it's possible that friends may come and go.

The important thing to remember is that we can't control how other people feel or think. We are not the boss of other people. We are only the boss of ourselves. If someone is consistently mean, we have to accept that they're being mean. Regardless of how much we want them to be nice to us, we can't force that to happen. Letting go of who we want a person to be and accepting who they really are is an important first step.

I need every child to see a rejection as a temporary position and an opportunity to find true friends. I want them to know that there IS a friendship group waiting for them. But they often can't find new friends while they are hanging onto people who don't value them. My advice to any young person who isn't accepted in a group: move on out of there!

Courage to be Human

It takes courage to let go of unrealistic expectations and genuinely love ourselves.

Andy was a self-confessed nerd who was obsessed with being the best. If he got anything less than an 'A' he felt like a failure.

He would study late into the night, reject social invitations and sometimes forget to eat because he was focussed on school work. Now, I know some parents out there are laughing to themselves, saying, 'Can I have a bit of Andy at my house please?'

But although Andy's ambition has merit, could he handle failure?

Perfectionists usually don't handle failure well, which makes the incredible talent they possess difficult to apply to real life situations. Perfectionism is different from the healthy pursuit of excellence. It is the pursuit of unrealistic standards.

In our culture, we love snapshot moments. It's all about the photographable. When our kids look good, win an award, smile, get along, it's easy to celebrate. However it is easy to elevate talents and forget the broader picture. I see this happen a lot with academically gifted students.

Parents think that if their children have everything else 'taken off them', they will be able to reach their potential. Their children may not have a part-time job or be required to help around the house. Because of their narrow focus they miss out on learning other essential life skills that will enable them to apply their talents in the real world. Too often I have seen these young people struggle to handle real life well.

When we parent with achievement in mind, we are unconsciously reinforcing perfectionism and don't prepare our children for real life. When we celebrate unrealistic standards at the expense of balanced, healthy ones, we can be guilty of pushing our kids to perform. These are examples of how parents unconsciously encourage perfectionism:

- Treating every exam like a life-altering moment.
- Doing their assignments for them.
- Being disappointed if they don't win or get a prize.
- Criticising them for small mistakes.
- Never being satisfied with the state of the house until it is perfect.
- Comparing them to other children or siblings.
- Dreaming big dreams for them.
- Controlling their every move.
- Continuing to push even if their child is overwhelmed.

Perfectionists have an 'all-or-nothing' mentality. They might say, 'I don't want to go to ballet anymore because I fell over in front of everyone!' or 'I messed up on my spelling test. I got two answers wrong!' When our children talk in terms of all or nothing, we have to help them find the grey. You might say, 'But all the other days you danced in time. Everyone has a bad day now and then.' Or, 'Eight right and two wrong. That doesn't sound like a disaster to me.'

It doesn't hurt for our children to fail occasionally and by doing so develop a tolerance for the realistic journey they will encounter as they pursue their dreams. In fact the ideal recipe for resilience is – small win, small win, fail, small win. Perfectionism doesn't accept this equation. If our children learn to fail well and adjust and get back up I know they will do well at whatever they put their hand to.

Take-home Tips:

- Aim to provide a childhood full of adventure. Life is meant to be a gritty adventure, rather than a walk in the park.

- Allow your child to experience, and see you experience, a full range of emotions. We do our children a great disservice when we over-protect them from experiencing negative emotions. Instead, we need to help our child become familiar with pain, fear, anger and sadness. My advice is to lean into strong emotion rather than away from it. This is the quickest way to help children navigate their way through it.

- Help your child to do five more squats when they think they have reached their capacity. We don't want our children to push past their emotional capacity to the point of burnout, but we *do* want them to know how to work with the burn and get another five squats out of themselves. In other words: don't squat them to death but stretch their capacity.

- Place value on your words and their impact. There is a real art to saying, 'I believe you can' creatively. The idea is to acknowledge pain while reminding young people of their strengths, abilities, relationships and innate worth.

- Be patient. It's understandable that our children may need repeat exposure to new things, and time to build resilience to them.

- Create time to invite and answer questions. If we don't create space for it, it may not happen.

- Teach them to know when and how to push back with truth loudly. If a child's family is a beacon of truth, it is far easier for them to recognise mistruths. It takes courage to tell others that they belong when they are being told they don't.

- Share stories about times you chose to stand alone. I need every child to see a rejection as a temporary position and an opportunity to find true friends.

- Accept that this is one of life's big and brutal concepts: people might choose not to like us. It's also possible that people might like you for a while and then change their mind. In other words, it's possible that your friends might come and go. We can't control how other people feel or think. We are not the boss of other people. We are only the boss of ourselves.

- Recognise if we are parenting out of misguided motives. When we celebrate unrealistic standards at the expense of balanced, healthy ones, we can be guilty of pushing our kids to perform.

Courage

Letting go of the ideal to embrace the real is hard sometimes, but it is important if we want to enjoy life as it presents itself. Gratitude says that whatever I have in my hands is enough.

2
GRATITUDE
Pick Up Your Shovel

Many years ago I taught a class that had significant learning needs. I watched children who struggled academically compare themselves with others. Some deeply resented their learning difficulties, whilst others strove to do their best despite their limitations. Children with a more positive mindset had usually found a non-academic passion or talent which they were very proud of and invested into.

I remember having a parent/teacher interview with a father whose child had a significant learning disability. Although his son was in Year 5, he was struggling to complete Year 2 work. Regardless of how hard he was pushed; his achievements would always be limited.

Like many of us, this father was seeing his child as a product of his parenting rather than a unique person in his own right. I spent a great deal of time talking to this dad about accepting his son for who he was and letting go of unrealistic expectations. At the time he was insisting on tutoring six days a week, but this was only exacerbating his son's feelings of inadequacy.

We have all, at times, been guilty of pushing our own agendas and expectations onto our children, instead of stepping back and fully appreciating and being grateful for who they are. We have the 'I wish' conversation in our minds, which is never based in gratitude. I wish she wasn't such a tomboy. I wish he was interested in sport. I wish they would speak up in public and not be so shy. To summarise: I wish they were more like me and less like them!

The dictionary defines 'gratitude' as a thankful appreciation for what an individual receives, whether tangible or intangible. When I read this definition, it makes me think of how grateful I need to be of who my children *are*, not who I *want* them to be. This is every parent's challenge.

Our children are gifts that need to be received with thankfulness. They need to hear the words, 'I wouldn't change you for the world'.

Each time we choose to be grateful for our kids, we teach them to love themselves. That is why first thing in the morning and last thing at night, I try to remind them how loved and valued they are. I want to tell them how much I am grateful for them, even when they have made mistakes or annoyed me! That's the time we all need to practise gratitude the most.

I also think it's good for our children to overhear us 'singing their praises', especially when they are going through hard times. Even if they are inflicting pain on the family, piercing their body in one hundred places or telling you how to run the world, we have to be careful that we don't vent unnecessary negativity on them. Our words are powerful. If your child has been in a lot of trouble lately, I suggest you get on the phone to their grandma and, in the loudest voice possible, talk about their finer qualities. They may think you are totally mad, but I'll let you in on a secret – they probably do already!

Gratitude is contagious. If we are thankful for our children, they are more likely to be thankful for themselves.

A Good Question to Ask

A good question for every caring adult to ask is, 'What are the expectations I should hold my children to?' I would rather hold my children accountable to the traits of resilience than specific achievements like high marks at school, because the traits of resilience will enable them to be the best version of themselves. Here are some great expectations that parents place value on:

Their work ethic, not wasting opportunities and being responsible for their own actions.

That they be kind.

Manners. Respect. Kindness. Empathy.

I think everything falls under the banner 'treat others how you want to be treated.'

I would always expect kindness, integrity, honesty and grit.

I believe expectations should always be achievable and realistic regarding responsibility for behaviour, respect for others, honesty and gratefulness.

To be thankful for what people do and the end goal of gratitude.

Love, mercy and being humble.

Loving and accepting yourself.

To be the best version of themselves.

And one mum fittingly suggested: *whatever expectations we hold them to, I think we need to be mindful and honest that we hold ourselves to those same expectations first.*

Gratitude's Link to Problem Solving

Years of research have consistently linked a person's overall happiness to their ability to be grateful. The benefits of gratitude have shown to affect the health of a person psychologically, physically and socially.

Robert Emmons' research, showcased in his book *Thanks!*, specifically talks about the social benefits of gratitude. Emmon talks about gratitude as a social strengthening emotion. Emmons' research discovered that when people are practising gratitude they are more responsive to other people. They themselves can become more helpful, outgoing, social, generous, compassionate, positive, and less isolated, less lonely, and less destructive.

I have personally witnessed one other great benefit of gratitude, which is best explained by telling you a story about my youngest son.

It was the school holidays. My 16-year-old son was staring into the pantry complaining he couldn't find anything to eat. Fifteen minutes passed. The complaining continued. I was working from home that day and literally had to step over him twice to get to our lounge room. He didn't know what he 'felt like' so he was lying on the kitchen floor, 'dying' of hunger. I am pretty sure he was hoping I would come to his rescue and whip him up a gourmet lunch. Has anyone else been summoned as a personal chef?

With every passing minute, the moaning got louder. With every passing minute, I got more annoyed. My son literally had nothing else to do that day except feed himself, whereas I was running around like a crazy lady trying to juggle the added pressure of school holidays on top of my usual workload. So, with a distinct tone of impatience I said, 'I don't want to hear it a minute longer. Just choose something. Get up and feed yourself. Stop making this a drama.'

My son is so articulate. In an instant he responded, 'Mum, it's just hard when this is the biggest problem in your life.'

I looked at his Nike shoes and fancy t-shirt. *'Wow'*, I thought. That is so true. The reason he was unable to decide what to eat was because gratitude was not at the foundation of his problem-solving process. He was thinking about what he *didn't* have rather than what he *did* have. I guarantee that if he had gone without food for a day, anything would have been adequate. For most of our kids, food is something they take for granted.

I have seen a lack of gratitude rob people of their problem-solving skills time and time again. Whether they are complaining about their school work, chores, not enough game time, an annoying little brother or not enough food options (even though the pantry is full!), it creates a mindset of *lack* rather than *possibility*. Although gratitude is not an instant fix or a miracle cure for problems, it helps us look forward.

If we choose to lean into challenges with gratitude, it enables us to explore opportunities more freely. Gratitude makes whatever we have in our hands enough. Our handful may not be everything we want or hope for, but it may be enough to solve the next problem at hand and make progress.

The power of gratitude doesn't stop there. Let's make it practical. Once you have this mindset, it needs to energise you to act. To solve problems we have to be prepared to do something! Be creative and take action in any number of positive ways – seeking support, investing in extra-curricular activities, using gratitude strategies at the meal table or making an appointment with a school teacher. Instead of using energy to complain, chanel energy into finding ways to make something work.

Real and Ideal at School

Megan was excited about her school excursion. She made sure she was first in line to get onto the bus, so she could get the best seat for her friends and herself. As soon as the doors opened, Megan raced to the front of the bus, sat behind the driver and motioned to her friends to join her. At the same time, someone else in her friendship group ran to get the back seat. Megan found herself sitting alone. Does anyone else remember a similar moment in their lives?

We have to teach our children that there is a difference between *real* and *ideal*. So often we all allow our ideal to spoil the real. We all have a dream of how we would like our day to unfold, but the reality may be different from this dream. Letting go of the ideal to embrace the real is really hard sometimes, but it is important if we want to enjoy life as it presents itself.

When the real happens, my advice is to respond to it. Don't spend a second wishing for the ideal. I have a suggestion for Megan: solve the problem. Either move to the back of the bus with your friends or stay and enjoy the people around you. The reality is this: things can turn out differently and still be enjoyable. If Megan is able to focus on what she has, not the minor thing that didn't go according to plan, she will have a much better day.

Another thing that I see rock children's worlds is not being placed in the same class group as their close friends. Simone, mother of a nine-year-old boy told me, 'My son had been in the same class group as his friends for three years before he was separated from them. We thought he was mentally prepared, but when he was getting dressed for the first day of school, it hit him

... and then he started crying.' It's hard for children to adapt to the real when they wish for the ideal.

Our children will face a range of social disappointments. Invitations that are not reciprocated can be one of these disappointments. You can hear children's pain when they say, 'I thought they were my friends, but they aren't.' Giving with the expectation of receiving something in return can really trip us up in life.

During these times parents can also hold too tightly to the ideal, which can lead them to interfere in inappropriate ways. I have seen many a mum ferociously fighting their child's battles for them, which seemed necessary at the time but in hindsight wasn't. Kayla said, 'I knew I shouldn't have done it, but I got my daughter's phone and pretended I was her. I texted her friend back telling her to, "Back off or I will tell my mum to talk to your mum." My daughter was asleep. I was so sick of her friend singling her out. I just wanted to put an end to it.'

I have also seen parents directly messaging children and try to 'pull them into line'. A guidance officer says, 'I am dealing with an incident now where a mother direct messaged another child and got into a catfight with them. You have to ask yourself who is the adult in situations like this. The mother called this girl the most horrific names, and regardless of whether she thought she was justified or not, it's completely inappropriate.'

Out of fear and an inability to focus on the big picture, parents can be lowering themselves to childish standards. I actually see a lot of this in Year 12 when parents know their child's friendship group well, and issues concerning formals, dating and schoolies' week are arising. I also see this in primary school, when mothers contact other mothers to sort out their children's friendship issues for them. It seldom helps. As I have said in my book *Parenting Teenage Girls in the Age of a New Normal*, exclusively parent your *own* child – not someone else's.

Our children are not going to learn how to handle their lives if we keep handling it for them. Squabbling children often end up mates again. Young people's worlds change a lot faster than ours do. Adults also take longer to apologise! I give parents the same advice I give children. Move on and move on quickly. Focus on what you can control and don't waste a second wishing for the ideal. Accept the real and respond to it, regardless of how unfair or difficult it is. Letting go of disappointments quickly can enable us to be grateful for the other things we have in life.

Our Home Environment

Optimism is a shield which does come more naturally to some than others. Not all of our children are blessed with a strong innate ability to see a 'glass half full'. Some young people have a genetically lower happiness 'set point' than others, and will therefore tend to see the negatives more easily. However, there are specific things we can do to help them along the way.

We can inject gratitude into our daily schedule intentionally by taking advantage of different times of the day. Bed time, meal time, travel time and personal time are all good times to boost gratitude. With practice, these can become times that our children anticipate and enjoy. Here are some suggestions as a starting point:

- **Bed time.** Too often our children go to bed debriefing about their daily problems instead of counting their blessings. Ideally, we should go to bed at night spending 5 to 15 minutes naming our blessings and thinking of the people, places, things and experiences that are beautiful in our lives. This enables our brains to be trained on a daily basis to see what is in our hands and at our disposal.

- **Meal time.** Helen, mother of four daughters, explains, 'We have a family habit of going around each person at the dinner table (we have four daughters; 9, 11, 14, 16) and saying 'what went well today?' It causes a sudden shift in everyone's attitudes, from the whining of 'this totally stank today', to seeing that good did happen. My girls need to see that they can always find something to be grateful for. It also helps us celebrate wins with each other. We find that on the days where we don't do this our home seems to be a more self-focused, negative environment.'

- **Travel time.** Before you listen to music, ask your child to describe three things they are grateful for. Other conversation starters may include, 'Tell me something that went well today', 'Tell me about someone you admire' or 'Talk to me about something that you are looking forward to.'

- **Technology time.** There are so many gratitude apps for smartphones that are excellent for kickstarting gratitude. They operate on the premise that if you are able to reflect in detail on the things you are grateful for each day, it will help you savour positive events and appreciate good things. I wish every teacher would inject this into their daily classroom routine, as I feel it is great use of educational time.

- **Quiet time.** Daily journaling is also powerful, especially if you are answering questions like 'if I woke up today with only the things I was grateful for yesterday, what would I wake up with?' Dream boards are another beautiful way to express gratitude and hope for the future. Gratitude walls, in the form of a blackboard in the kitchen or meal area, are another way for families to express gratitude. These are places for children to collate images, ideas and quotes that are great visual reminders that their lives are valuable and blessed.

Don't Rush Gratitude

It's a challenge to spend time 'in gratitude'. Most families live a fast-paced life. Tossing a quick thank you via text isn't always being grateful; it is ticking another thing off our list. I personally wonder if the pace of our lives stops our children truly connecting with their blessings and experiencing gratitude on a profound level.

I am not sure about you, but successes usually energise me. I receive a buzz that motivates me for 'what's next?' I feel like I am wasting time by staying and celebrating the moment for too long. I feel empowered and ready to run, and the last thing I want to do is be slowed down.

What if I were to propose that by investing more time into the 'thank you process', you would give yourself and your children a double gift? Not only would they have the blessing of what they received but they would also receive a positive outlook on life.

I believe the longer we spend in the 'thank you' process, the more we are affected by it.

It is easy to rush through 'thank you' moments that are meant to be savoured.

Challenging our children to express their appreciation for family and friends 'in their own words' can really cement gratitude. Thank you notes, acts of service and kind words are all ways we can take time to express appreciation. I love it when my boys voluntarily get up and start doing the dishes after I have cooked a really nice family meal. That is their way of saying 'thank you'. It does me good and it does them good.

Emma Scout, mother of three, explains how she teaches gratitude in her home when she says, 'I find if I acknowledge "what" I am grateful for, the response from my children is different. Instead of saying a closed "thanks", I say, "Thanks for bringing the clothes in. I really appreciate it as I had a big day and I can now relax instead of doing housework." When I do this my children truly understand that I am grateful, and a really lovely vibe becomes present. I also notice if I use this language, then so do they.'

Remember, small blessings in our lives might not feel noteworthy, but they are. Noticing a small contribution from a family member is just as important as noticing a larger one. It's common to significantly underestimate the small moments and overestimate the 'Instagrammable'. It is easy to be wanting the next photo-worthy moment while underestimating how valuable some of the small, seemingly insignificant things are. Similarly, a favourite colour, a smell, the weather, the shape of a leaf or the chirp of a bird can all be undervalued if we don't stop to appreciate them with our children.

The 'Give Up' Strategy

It is not difficult to notice times when authentic gratitude is lacking in our homes. I have come to recognise that an indulgent life doesn't make kids happy. The 'Give Up' strategy is a quick gratitude booster that any family can use when gratitude is lacking. It requires us to take something away from our children's lives, either physically or mentally, until their appreciation for it increases again.

Familiarity blind sights many of us. Sometimes imagining something is gone is enough to make you appreciate it. I know someone who imagines every day that their loved ones die so he doesn't take them for granted. I am not sure if I would want to visualise my husband and kids dying each day, but every now and then it pays to stop and take stock of what life would feel like if they were gone.

The 'Give Up' strategy reminds me of the way I used to rotate my children's toys when they were little. I had about three groups of toys which I would swap regularly. Two would stay in the cupboard, packed away, until the novelty had worn off the ones they were currently playing with. Each time I brought a different set of toys down from the cupboard, it felt like Christmas. I always found when they had too many toys, they lost interest in all of them. We make it hard for our children to be grateful by giving them too much.

We might try and use the 'Give Up' strategy with our kids by saying, 'If you aren't thankful, I am going to take that away.' Research actually suggests that this is not a bad idea. We can temporarily give up something and then reintroduce it at a later date. If our children were to spend a few weeks a year living with someone else, or in a third world country, it would undoubtedly boost their appreciation for what they do have at home.

A perfect time to use the 'Give Up' strategy is when our children don't take care of their belongings. For example, if your child has an iPhone and a case, but they decide to take it out of the case and it accidently gets smashed on the ground, the 'Give Up' strategy might help. Giving up a phone for a while may help them take care of it next time. The same may apply if they keep losing something you paid for. Don't jump in and financially bail them out, as that approach won't teach gratitude.

This is a powerful truth to remember: our children will eventually lose what they aren't grateful for.

Challenging Ungratefulness

I have noticed that parents are reluctant to talk about gratitude with young people who are going through hard times. However, I believe our reluctance does them a great disservice. Even in those times it is important to lovingly challenge an unhealthy mindset, remembering this really is their 'first rodeo' and they can't see beyond their fears.

About a year ago I was approached by a mother of three. Her youngest daughter had a disability. Tegan, her 13 year old, had built up some resentment about the amount of time her mother was spending with her younger disabled sister. She was also embarrassed that her family was different, and she was angry she couldn't bring people home comfortably. Any family who has a child with a disability knows how tough it can be. It had to be acknowledged.

Tegan was surrounded by girlfriends who were cutting. She had very, very tiny scratches on her thighs. She was – understandably – crying for attention. Her mother was terrified that self-harm was going to take hold of her daughter and was responding with all guns blazing. She was the best mother a girl could have.

We met and talked. Mum cried. I thought about offering suggestions like 'take your daughter out by herself once a week', 'buy her a bracelet to remind her how loved she is', or 'write her a meaningful letter'. And all those things could have been said, but my guess was that her mother was already doing all those things and there was still a gaping hole. Usually mums end up talking to me once they have tried the obvious!

To the parents who are out there reading this book: I know you have tried all the obvious things. I get it. All the common-sense things just aren't working – or at least, not quickly. Sometimes it's not simple; 2 + 2 doesn't always add up to 4. Just acknowledging that is important.

I remember sending mum out of the room and sitting alone with this dear girl. I prepared her for a tough conversation by saying this, 'I want you to promise me that at the end of this conversation you and I are still going to be friends.' That was the best way I knew how to say, 'Things are about to get awkward.' She was ready to talk, so it made it easy for me to have a direct conversation.

For the next 45 minutes I told her that I couldn't, in good conscience, tell her that she had a life that was worth cutting away. I reminded her that the mum who was in the waiting room loved her more than life itself; that she had a roof over her head, food on the table and a school that would bend over backwards to support her. Small things in a privileged society, but worth noting.

I promised her that the way forward would not be found by focusing on her disappointment, regardless of how deep those disappointments were. Then we had a marshmallow break! We were still friends. In fact, she was smiling. It's amazing what a bit of truth said in love can do to inspire someone's heart.

We also spoke about the benefit that her disappointments could bring to her life. Finding benefits in disappointments is like finding gold. To find the gold she would have to wade into the darkest of areas, find a shovel and deliberately dig. I truly believe that if young people can take their toughest moment, and find gratitude in THAT moment, gratitude will be their secret for future successes.

Parents, I know we want to hand our child a perfect, trouble-free life – but we can't. Whether it be a divorce, bankruptcy or health issue, real life seldom looks perfect. It's impossible to sidestep heartache. However, I believe that the very hardships you would prefer to rescue them from could be the secret to your child's happiness.

Gratitude Makes Everything Enough

Am I grateful for struggles? No. I can't say that I am. I can't be grateful for pain, suffering or illness. Neither am I grateful for

Gratitude

abuse, poverty or evil. If I were to talk to a young person who had suffered due to another's wrongdoing, I wouldn't ask them to be grateful for the actual event. That would be absurd. However, as the saying goes, every cloud has a silver lining. I believe that a silver lining is there for us to discover. It's not hardship that we are thankful for, but the lessons that come from the hardship.

I believe that real life (not their ideal life) is enough for our children to find happiness in. If I didn't believe this, I would have given up hope a long time ago. I have seen young people and families go through some incredibly tough times and come out the other side with a strong sense of hope and determination for their future. It *is* possible.

I gave Tegan a gratitude journal that helped her identify things she could be thankful for every day: things that may already be passing through her mind that she wasn't fully appreciating. We had to train her brain to focus on positives. Sometimes she felt like the journal was annoying and silly, and other times she saw value in it. Most of us feel like this when we start practising gratitude.

Tegan and I began to meet every week, and that's when we really started digging for gold. I helped her pick up her shovel. Piece by piece, gem by gem, we found treasure. I wanted to help her find what made her life special, unique and valuable to the world. Why did she want to be a part of her family and no one else's?

Some weeks we made progress and other weeks it felt as if we didn't. The most beautiful revelation that Tegan had was that she didn't want to be anyone else's daughter. Why? Tegan decided that her mum was the only mum who could teach her courage, strength and love. She was grateful for her mum, and glad to belong to her mum. That right there made a huge difference! That was her turning point. Gratitude requires maturity – but once discovered, it works for the long haul.

Gratitude transformed how she viewed her mother and interacted with her family, making her more aware of the positives and also her ability to contribute to the home. In a generation that has been called 'entitled', we must cultivate gratitude as a defence against the destructive thinking that wants to rob young people of seeing the love that surrounds them.

Take-home Tips:

- Remember gratitude is contagious.

- Accept your child, just as they are without trying to improve or fix them. Each time we choose to be grateful for our kids, we teach them to love themselves. If we are thankful for our children, they are more likely to be thankful for themselves.

- Teach your children that there is a difference between real and ideal. Letting go of the ideal to embrace the real is really hard sometimes, but it is important if we want to enjoy life as it presents itself.

- Respond to life the way it presents itself. When the real happens, don't spend a second wishing for the ideal.

- Inject gratitude into your daily schedule intentionally by taking advantage of bed time, meal time, travel time and personal time. These times can become times that our children anticipate and enjoy.

- Note small blessings. A favourite colour, a smell, the weather, the shape of a leaf or the chirp of a bird can all be undervalued if we don't stop to appreciate them with our children.

- Think before gifting. We make it hard for our children to be grateful by giving them too much.

- Don't be afraid to use the 'Give Up' strategy. Our children will eventually lose what they aren't grateful for.

- Remember that it is impossible to sidestep heartache. We can't hand our children a perfect, trouble-free life. However, I believe that the very hardships you would prefer to rescue your children from could be the secret to their happiness.
- Recognise gratitude's power. We must cultivate gratitude as a defence against the destructive thinking that wants to rob young people of seeing the love that surrounds them.

Gratitude

You don't have to agree with a person to practise empathy. The more empathetic you are, the easier it will be to put yourself in the shoes of people who are different than you.

Empathy enables our children to see things from another person's perspective. Without empathy, young people won't be able to see things from their friend's, sibling's or parent's perspective.

3
EMPATHY
The Cost of Caring

Courtney is nine. She's has had the same tight-knit group of friends since preschool. Some would call them 'a clique'. Others would call them 'the popular girls'. No one has come or gone from their group in the five years they have been at school together. Yet, one day a fresh-faced new girl unassumingly sits down with them at lunchtime. The awkwardness is tangible, and the body language of the girls announce that they are an 'invitation only' group. Soon after, the new girl shuffles on and things return to business as normal.

I wish I could convince every 'cliquey group' to follow their inner prompt of empathy. I often talk to girls about getting really good at making people feel special by having a great welcoming strategy. Simple statements like, 'Hello, it's great to see you here!' can go a long way to welcoming a new comer. Because communication is 70% body language, gestures like moving over to make space for someone and smiling all help newcomers feel welcome. Ideally, what girls should never do is ignore them, turn their back or exclude them from conversations.

It has to be acknowledged that the dynamics in boys' friendship groups are different than in girls' groups. When I talk to boys about girls' friendship issues, most just roll their eyes. Boys need to find common ground to make friends, whereas girls can have all the common ground in the world and still be enemies. Common ground is usually based around an interest or activity, like technology, sport, gaming or dinosaurs. A boy will more easily pass someone a ball or have a laugh with a new person, without 'sussing them out' first or even needing to have a lengthy conversation. If the other child can catch the ball, they are in.

The dynamics of boys' groups are more inclusive and less structured. This is not to say that boys' groups aren't without their issues; they are just different issues. Dominant boys can be aggressive, easily irritated, loud, boisterous and physically stronger. Boy banter can be brutal and difficult for more sensitive boys to handle. Boys' empathy can also be very difficult to locate. They are often oblivious (and sometimes not so oblivious) to how harsh their words are or how unkind they are being.

Inside Someone's Shoes

Empathy is an appreciation of another person's point of view, feelings and state of mind. It has been defined as a person's capacity to place themselves inside the shoes of another and see the world through their eyes. You don't have to agree with a person or be like them to practise empathy. The more empathetic you are, the easier it will be to put yourself in the shoes of people who are different from you.

Researchers have identified a range of moral principles relating to empathy such as caring, defending, comforting, respect, compassion, fairness, perspective taking and avoidance of harm. All are critical in positive social interactions and make a huge contribution to society in general. Schools hold empathy as a guidepost for all student interactions. Restorative practices and anti-bullying programs nurture empathy. Awards for kindness, consideration and care all promote empathy as an honourable trait.

Although empathy might seem a strange topic to talk about in a book about resilience, research makes a clear link. Young people who show more empathy are better connected, more likely to withstand social trauma well, more likely to resolve and less likely to escalate social conflict.

Without empathy, we wouldn't exist. We would destroy each other and ourselves. For this reason it has to be concluded that taking care of those weaker and more vulnerable than yourself is a natural feeling. However, current research suggests that 30 years ago, we were showing 30% more empathy in our daily lives. It also points towards technology as one reason we have a less empathetic society. You don't learn empathy through texting or rushing past people or being surrounded by raging gamers. You learn empathy by taking time to connect with people and listen to them.

Knowledge of the process by which young people acquire empathy is limited and is thought to be influenced by both biological and environmental factors including upbringing. When it comes to children and adolescents, developmental stages have a great deal to do with how much empathy they show. MRI's have shown that the structural changes that take place in the brain during adolescence affect young people's social interactions. Taking that into consideration, it is evident that young people are less likely to be masters of empathy and more likely to need coaching to develop it.

One of the signs that young people are growing up is their ability to ask questions and put themselves in the shoes of another person. The ability to be 'others orientated' can take some young people longer than others to develop. The first time your high-school aged child or young adult asks, 'Do you need a hand cooking dinner, Mum?' is a sign that things are improving.

Empathy

As Nichole put it: 'The default is for everyone to think about themselves, especially teenagers, because they don't think that anyone is going through what they are going through. They think they are the only ones. They don't realise that there are 20 million other teenagers in the world who are also having a hard time at school! My 20-year-old is finally starting to sound like she has some perspective about what others experience.'

Modelling Empathy

It is critical that we take advantage of opportunities to model empathy every day; whether that be to show kindness when it is undeserved or to take time to fully understand before we respond. Our children notice gestures like helping an old person return their trolley or smiling at a stranger. Modelling empathy should be on the forefront of our mind every day – not just as an afterthought. As Ken Ginsburg rightly says, 'Nothing we say is as important as what we do.'

One key time we can show empathy is when our children are being disrespectful. It is easy to think we are more empathetic than we really are. It is easy to show kindness when our children's point of view is the same as ours, when they are doing what we ask or meeting our expectations. However, it is far more difficult when we feel angry or disappointed with them and their behaviour.

How we speak to our child does a great deal to help them understand empathy. We often forget how vulnerable they are to our emotions. Our children are far more likely to respect us if we say 'no' from a position of understanding their distress, fear or frustration. Similarly, teachers who say 'no' with empathy are more likely to be well received by students than those who don't. Fair yet firm is a good guide.

Another way we can practise empathy is by asking questions rather than making assumptions. The extent to which adults listen to children is a good indication of empathy. When we say things such as, 'I bet you haven't even cleaned that room yet?' or 'You didn't really eat those vegetables, did you?' or 'Don't give me excuses', we are not building respect. Judgemental statements using 'always' and 'never' don't model empathy. Watch out for off-handed comments such as, 'He never helps around the house,' or 'I doubt he's finished his assignment,' or 'You always end up breaking things'.

As parents, we need to take responsibility for altering our own negative language before we ask our children to. We need to ask ourselves: *Do I speak and behave in ways that will bring out the best in my child? Do I offer an opportunity to change – or only a dead-end conclusion? Do my messages show understanding?* Even the most well-meaning parents need to monitor this from time to time.

Self-Centred Siblings

Although sibling rivalry is developmentally very normal, it can cause children a lot of pain if empathy is not in the mix. Most parents deal with their children constantly checking that treats are distributed equally between them. However, there are some siblings who take this rivalry to the extreme, competing and hurting each other regularly and on purpose. Harsh words and judgements can do great damage. For this

Empathy

reason, it is important we keep empathy in the forefront of their relationships.

Denise, a mother of twins, spoke to me about the rivalry between them, 'All of my children are quite competitive, but in particular my identical twin daughters who are 13 years old – from the moment they realised they could be rivals to fight for our attention until now, when they are comparing school marks, sporting achievements and Instagram likes. They love each other dearly but they always seem to want to compare themselves to the other. I have always encouraged them to be individuals, but I think being identified by others as twins means they want to stand out against the other twin.'

Ray also says, 'Boys get to an age when they want to be the best. It's like their ego gets out of control! They can be really competitive with each other, belittling and lording it over those younger than them. I notice that my son even tries to do this with me sometimes!'

As I have spoken to groups of young adults about sibling rivalry, it has been interesting to hear their responses:

Sara, 18, says, *My sister was 14 months younger. She always wanted to do everything I was doing. She would always say 'it's not fair'. When I got an iPhone, she got one at the same time ... I had to push so hard to get one and then she just got one handed to her. I felt like I had to earn everything, and she was spoilt rotten. The younger one gets all the attention. You feel like you have to be the best or win just to stand out.*

Britt, 19, says, *My brother doesn't have to do his homework straight after he gets home like I did, and his room is never tidy. They have different standards with him than they did with me. It is hard to have a good relationship with someone who gets favoured.*

Amy, 17, says, *I was the middle child. I have a brother who is two years old and then twins two years younger. Getting Mum's attention was practically impossible and I knew it. It sucks when you want something, and you know it can't happen. My mum had to look after the little ones. Looking back, I realise that I used to cry for no reason, just so I could get a hug from her.*

Melissa, 20, says, *You learn different ways to get the attention that you need. You learn to help around the house or get the little kids into bed sooner, so that Mum might have time to ask me how my day was. I used to think, 'If I help my mum with this baby, I might get what I need.'*

Young people might feel that their siblings have more friends, more opportunities, more attention, or are more favoured by their parents. In many cases I have to agree with them. Life – with all its complexities – is often unfair. However, I believe that letting go of injustices, whether small or great, takes empathy – the capacity to put yourself in the shoes of someone else. Without empathy, young people won't be able to see things from their sibling's or parent's perspective.

There is nothing abnormal about sibling rivalry. It can be difficult when children are discovering themselves at different paces. One could be charging ahead successfully, while another could be floundering. It's only over time that young people realise that they can't be 'up' all the time. Everyone has successful and less successful seasons. For all our children, finding their unique place in the world is often a struggle to discover.

Empathy

Ideally, we want to create a home environment where children feel their needs are acknowledged and responded to. 'What do you need from me?' or 'How can I help?' is something I find myself asking my children regularly. When we are able to acknowledge and respond to what our children need, a lot of the related competition dissolves. We want to reassure them that they don't have to compete to have their needs met.

Putting yourself in someone else's shoes rarely happens in the heat of an argument. It is only when two open-hearted people come together to listen, instead of talking, that it is able to happen. This takes maturity. When we say to our children, 'Everyone else has feelings just like you. What would your brother or sister be feeling?' we alert them to use empathy. Sometimes our children can't get past their own feelings, but we need to keep giving them the option.

Structured family meetings may provide younger siblings the support to express their feelings to older siblings in a constructive and impacting way. I have encouraged families whose children are 'always' fighting to structure weekly communication time, where parents facilitate understanding and cooperation. Sometimes our children need us to intervene in this way. In some cases, a counsellor or psychologist can be brought in to help a family establish better ways of relating.

We also need to understand the importance of saying 'no'. If we give our children what they want or demand all the time, we are doing them a disservice. Being more lenient on a little one at the expense of an older ones – or vice versa – can cause problems. Having a favourite or treating our children differently based on gender is also unhelpful. It takes empathy to listen to our children's perspectives and needs, and respond accordingly.

Handling Aggression

Throughout my career I have met many young people who have suffered extreme bullying. One 7-year-old boy, who attended Youth Excel's Psychology Clinic, had his back fractured by 10-year-old boys who stomped on him after school. The police supervised the school for months after in order to prevent another incident.

An 8-year-old girl had her head flushed in the toilet by a peer daily, and was repeatedly pushed, shoved and excluded in the most savage and sneaky fashion I have ever seen. The long-term damage for this child was horrible and not easily repaired.

I recently spent time with a family whose daughter who had been diagnosed with mild Asperger's syndrome. Tahlia was getting teased in Year 7, but in year 8 and 9 things got really nasty quickly. She was receiving daily texts and emails from classmates, which included photos of ugly dogs with comments like, 'That's you with make-up on' and 'That's your face in 20 years.' This dear girl said, 'I tried putting my hair in a bow every day and wearing make-up to school to say I was a new person.' She didn't want to get on her computer or phone after school because she didn't want to see the messages. It was horrid behaviour but difficult for her to share with adults.

When Tahlia shared her experiences with her mum, she understandably wanted to march straight up to the principal's office the minute she found out. However, I encouraged her to wait and be more calculated about reporting the incidents. Schools can only act on fact, so if she could collect screen shots and daily records of behaviour for at least two weeks, she would be more likely to give the school what they needed to improve the situation rather than create a dust storm.

Bullying is when aggression is used to achieve particular goals to gain dominance over others. This dominance may not be physical but psychological or social. It is defined by the intention, repetition and imbalance of power.

Those who have experienced bullying are ten times more likely to bully others. In the coming months or years after bullying, children may fly off the handle quickly, responding to texts and messages inappropriately, or even becoming physically involved in fights more quickly than before. This overreaction can happen when our children don't process things that have been out of their control. They become triggered to hurt others and themselves.

In contrast, children who are supported by caring adults can develop empathy instead of bitterness. Children can gain hidden treasure in the darkest times of their lives. Processing pain well is the quickest way to find that treasure. Mia's story is a perfect example of this:

Mia attended a large state high school on the outskirts of Brisbane, Australia. After lunch, Mia was talking to her teacher about her school work before class began. Everything was business as normal. Many students were coming through the classroom door and taking their seats.

Then one of her classmates randomly came through the classroom door, pushed Mia backwards and pulled her over three rows of desks by her hair (yes – directly in front of the teacher!) It was then that one of the boys in the class came to the rescue and pulled the girl off Mia.

The teacher quickly grabbed Mia and held her close until the office collected her and called her mother. Her mother phoned me after the incident in absolute shock and horror over the physical violence. What added to the distress was that the girl was not expelled, and Mia was faced with the challenge of returning to school and seeing her again.

Prior to this incident, Mia and this girl had never spoken. There was no prior history of friendship issues. She wasn't dating her ex-boyfriend, and she hadn't 'uninvited' her to a party on the weekend. It was simply a case of one girl having a bad day and taking it out on an innocent bystander.

The school offered empathy training for the aggressive girl and mediation for the two of them, at which Mia was to receive an apology. Mia was afraid to attend. She didn't want to resolve things with someone who clearly had no respect for her. She wanted to move schools and never have to see the girl again!

Research has consistently shown that a lack of control over a situation damages people's ability to thrive. This had been an incident over which Mia had no control. I wanted to put some control back in her hands by allowing her the time she needed to process what had happened. Over the next few months, Mia's mother and I guided her to process her feelings using these four important lessons. She did return to school which was awesome, and she was also able to face her bully with empathy and strength.

Four Important Lessons

These are four things that I would recommend a parent speak to their child about after trauma. I have written this as if I were

Empathy

speaking them to Mia herself. These are my suggestions to build resilience and promote empathy during incidents of bullying:

1. Justice is important. Some things aren't right and should not be tolerated by society – or you! That is why we have rules to govern behaviour. There is *no* time when it is okay to hurt another human being.

2. Wounds are real. When someone hurts us, we feel wounded. You might not feel like yourself for a short while, but it is my job to comfort and support you. I want you to express and talk about your pain as much as you need to. You will also find ways to support and comfort yourself. This, rather than ignoring or avoiding pain, is your best and quickest way to feeling strong again.

3. You are powerful. You are strong enough to get through this and become stronger for it. Real strength is not about dominating someone else but controlling your own reactions. Ask yourself, what can you control and what actions can you take? We (mum, dad, your teachers, friends) believe you have great strength as a person. It's okay to take time to find this strength.

4. Would you really want to trade places? When you think about the person who hurt you, I want you to try and put yourself in their shoes. Their shoes might not fit you, but it's a good idea to walk around in them for a while. Can you imagine what might drive someone to act like that? How they might they be feeling now? Where their future might take them if they don't choose different behaviour?

The Cost of Caring

There is a lot of talk these days about kindness and its positive impact on people's happiness. I often feel as if people are trying to sell kindness by promising outrageous benefits to those who use it. I don't subscribe to the idea that self-motived, small acts of kindness, bring returns in bucket loads. My concept of kindness and those sold in glossy magazines is quite different.

Acts of kindness come from a place of empathy. I have often expressed kindness after my heart was broken by someone else's problem, circumstance or challenges. Allowing your heart to be involved on that level is a choice. A person has to be open to the possibility that their own life will be disrupted.

I have noticed that there is a cost associated with kindness that many don't want to incur. In my life, acts of kindness have often come at a great personal expense. Not only have they taken time and effort, but emotional energy that, once spent, can't be reclaimed. While I fully believe the impact on my happiness and wellbeing is real, I acknowledge that you have to be prepared to invest selflessly for it to bring returns.

When I see young people motivated to be kind to one another, I truly admire them. Whether they pick up someone's hat in the playground, let someone through a door first, help someone with their school work or refrain from gossiping, they are thinking of the interests of others. Let's notice and praise acts of kindness!

No act of kindness is small when it is intentional.

I love this statement by Pastor Wintley Phipps: 'Your best destiny is the moment you most resemble, reflect and reveal

Empathy

the character of God.' I asked my Facebook community to tell me the kindest thing they had ever seen their child do. These responses are just beautiful and reassure me that our children do have the capacity to empathise and show kindness everyday:

My son gave his tuckshop money to a little boy in the playground who sat alone and was sad. He was a stranger to my son. It was the money my son had been given by the tooth fairy. He went without and he gave all the money away. Melted my heart.

My eldest daughter asked me to stop the car in the pouring rain so she could get out and ask an elderly lady if she would like a lift home.

My 4-year-old and I bought a four-pack of lollies while his brothers were at school. He put one packet in his oldest brother's drawer knowing it was his favourite, two in his second oldest brother's drawer because they were his favourite flavours, and saved one for himself. I wasn't sure he would want to share any of them! This is a very big deal!

My son gently and lovingly escorts my mother in so many situations. Such a gentleman.

We were at Aldi and this older lady was in front of us and was very flustered. My son is young, so I was dealing with him and trying to give the lady her space. My daughter walked passed me, pulled out her wallet and gave the lady $3. She was exchanging dog food and she was $3 short, and had forgotten her debit card. My daughter said, 'What if that was your grandma? Would you still act like this?' to an impatient and rude lady behind us. I was floored!

My grandma is a widow and turning 90 this year. This year, my daughter set up a whole agenda for dinner and a movie. She then worked with her the next day at the library she volunteers at. It really made my grandma's summer to know that my now 13-year-old would want to spend time with an old lady. They had fajitas and watched The Blues Brothers.

My son offered to give all his savings to his twin because she wants a 'Go Pro', and he doesn't need his money as he doesn't want to buy anything.

Alex is only two. The other day I had a bug, was lying in bed feeling awful, and he came running in to lay beside me and pat my face. He left a bowl of chips and a chocolate biscuit in the lounge room.

My son is in grade 5. While on an excursion in the city, he walked up to a homeless man and gave him his lunch. This prompted other kids to do the same. From this act of kindness, a blanket drive was run at the school to assist the homeless.

I didn't see it, but my son played with a girl at school for a week because it was her birthday. While the class was singing 'Happy Birthday', all the boys refused to sing because they thought she was 'too fat', so my son sang loudly and played with her. He told his friends that he could not be friends with people who were mean to others because of what they looked like.

The Great Balance

It is difficult for our children to know how to handle the empathy they feel, and as a result they often become over invested. Supporting friends with mental illness and any range of real-life issues can be tough on kids. They truly do the job of counsellors and more on some days. They do a remarkable job! However, being over-involved and experiencing what is termed 'empathy distress' is not productive for anyone.

When I talk to young people about caring for friends, I use an image of a man riding a bike in the middle of a crowded street, with a load on his back that is 100 times bigger than the bike itself. It helps open a discussion about carrying unrealistic burdens. It's easy to get worried about other people's problems or friendship issues to your own detriment.

I recently got a call from a mum whose daughter was worried sick about a friend who had run away from home. She was furiously texting her, trying to find out where she had gone. The intensity increased as the night wore on. I advised her daughter to send her friend the phone numbers of a few trusted adults and at least one Helpline. This would send a clear message that she felt unqualified to handle such an 'adult size' issue.

Here are some thoughts to help every young person who is supporting a friend who is struggling.

Things Friends Should Do:

- Listen and care about your friend's feelings but then move on and talk about normal things.
- Plan to do normal activities together.
- Look after yourself as a priority. Your sleep and study time is important.

- Encourage your friend to get professional support if they don't already. You may want to go with them to a school counsellor to help them take that step.
- Make a pact with your friend that allows you to contact an adult (who you both agree on) if you are ever concerned about their safety.
- If you receive a message or an image that disturbs you, screen shot it and contact an adult.
- Never promise not to tell an adult.

Things Friends Shouldn't Do:

- Try to be your friend's parent or counsellor.
- Push confessions or conversations about problems.
- Increase the drama by talking to others about their problems.
- Show other friends text messages or images.

The Power of Pets

Josiah had a difficult first year of high school. His family had moved interstate, and he had not found making friends at his new school easy. His usually happy-go-lucky nature disappeared and he became quiet and withdrawn. As time passed, his parents discovered he was also being bullied, but because Josiah didn't want to talk about details, they never knew exactly what was going on. They did, however, guess that without a solid peer group to support him, his mood was unlikely to improve.

On a whim, and hoping to put a smile on his face, they bought him a pet dog as a surprise gift. Josiah had always wanted a dog, but his mum hadn't. She liked her new, clean house and saw a dog as a big inconvenience. But desperate times called for desperate measures! His parents were looking for any way to help their son find happiness.

Benji – as this dog became known – brought more benefits to Josiah than his parents had ever anticipated. This dog became Josiah's lifeline. Benji became his comfort and support when he felt like there was not another human who would understand him. Over a few weeks his parents noticed he was calmer and more communicative and they were finally able to get inside his world and find out what was troubling him.

Josiah's mum credited all that to his dog. She swears by pets for children because she has experienced first-hand the impact they can have. The research agrees with Josiah's mum. Having a relationship with a pet can help a child develop responsibility, empathy, care and communication. Pets can provide comfort, support and confidence during difficult times. They help children with development, family harmony and even their health. Children with pets have higher self-esteem, improved social skills, are more likely to be physically active and less likely to be overweight. They learn to look after something other than themselves. That's a lot of pluses!

At times when our young people (especially boys) start to physically pull away from parents, animals can be a good option to cuddle and pat. The rhythm of stroking a pet and feeling a pet's breath go in and out, can be comforting for children. Not having to talk, but just being accepted and needed by a pet is a really special gift.

These parents also share their experiences with pets:

George explains, *We have a beautiful dog named Rosey and when my boy Joshua was young he used to get night terrors so we would put Rosey on the end of his bed. His night terrors were less frequent and he would have a sound sleep; we often found her snuggled up beside him.*

Maria explains, *I got my young children a dog after a bad separation; all three children were under four at the time. It was the best therapy for them. They would cuddle and talk to her, and she would sleep on the end of their beds. Even now the children are 10, 11 & 13 and will still do it. She follows them around and gets excited to see them after school. Now that I am very sick she stays close to me and can even pick up when I'm about to have a bad episode before I do. When the ambulances have to come she WILL not leave my side. Getting a dog was the best $150 I ever spent.*

Take-home Tips:

- Realise that the ability to be 'others orientated' can take some young people longer than others to develop. Our children's default is to think about themselves.

- Practise and model empathy by asking questions rather than making assumptions. The extent to which adults listen to children is a good indication of empathy.

- Alert your child to the fact that other people have feelings by asking them, 'What might your sister or brother be feeling?' Without empathy, young people won't be able to see things from their sibling's or parent's perspective.

- Teach empathy in family meetings. Structured family meetings may provide younger siblings the support to express their feelings to older siblings in a constructive and impacting way.

- Use the '4 Important Lessons' to help a young person process rather than ignore pain.

- Quietly praise acts of kindness, as they have their own reward. Remember that no act of kindness is small when it is intentional.

- Help young people understand that there is a cost associated with kindness. It may not always be comfortable.

- Clearly define what a good friend is and isn't, and how best to support friends who are struggling with their mental health. This is a conversation about emotional boundaries we need to have regularly with our children as many young people don't know how to handle the empathy they possess.

- Consider a pet. At times when our young people (especially boys) start to physically pull away from parents, animals can be a good option to cuddle and pat. The rhythm of stroking a pet, feeling a pet's breath go in and out, can be comforting for children.

Empathy

*It's easy to reward exceptional talent.
The biggest or most visible talents are often
falsely perceived as the best. In contrast, the
smallest talents can produce big rewards for each
child who uses them. Fully-developed small
talents make big contributions to the world.*

4
SELF-AWARENESS
Big is Found in Little

From a very young age I had a clear understanding of my strengths and sense of purpose. It might sound strange to some, but even in my early years of primary school, I remember daydreaming about speaking in front of crowds of people. At 12 I was writing my first book, which I was sure was going to be a best seller. Once I had a glimpse of what my life was going to look like, I held onto it tightly. I didn't want to let it go. The more I looked at it, experimented with it and pursued it, the clearer the picture of who I was and what I could contribute became.

What was formulating in my mind and heart as a child was a life saver in the years to come. It helped me stay 'on track' during the most challenging of my growing up years. Because I could hear (and internally see) my purpose so clearly, people's negative opinions rarely found a permanent place in my heart. When people suggested, 'I couldn't' or 'I wouldn't', it was difficult to believe them. Purpose gave me inner knowledge that bypassed negativity or misguided feedback. Try as I might to give them power in my life, I just couldn't.

There were many opportunities to divert from the future that I saw. The career I would choose (at the time interior design looked a lot more glamorous than teaching) and what friends I would hang out with weren't easy decisions. These were times when I chose my purpose over comfort. Some of these decisions were difficult, but I found it was more difficult to turn my back on my purpose than to choose a counterfeit.

Purpose guides life decisions, influences behaviour, shapes goals, offers a sense of direction, and creates meaning. For me it did all of these and more. Whenever I discarded my purpose I felt lost. Finding myself again was as easy as coming back to my life's purpose and making decisions based on that. If it was dark and I was unsure of where to go, my life's purpose was the light that helped me know where to put my foot. I began to discover the reward that came from following my strengths and dreams in life. It brought me joy that external things or popularity couldn't give me.

To me, life's purpose is innate – and then nurtured. No one could give my life's purpose to me because I believe I was born with it. People could encourage or discourage it, but they couldn't give it to me. Father Richard Rohr describes it as 'the face I had before I was born'. Because no one gave it to me, no one can take it away. Because I was born with it, I will die with it. My purpose has been the immovable amongst the shifting sand.

Every person needs their own unique reason to get up in the morning. They need something that brings them joy, and that motivates them to keep going in the face of adversity. For some, this is connected to their vocation, and for others it is not. Regardless, I genuinely believe that every single person has a reason for living that is unique – a reason that, once discovered, can shout louder to them than any challenge or person's opinion ever could.

This discovery is what I want for your children and mine.

Cultivating Self-Awareness

Research suggests that people without purpose struggle to make decisions, stay motivated, be confident and happy. This is why I am genuinely concerned about the number of young adults who are travelling through life without a sense of purpose to guide them. It makes me really sad to see young people who are unable to articulate their skills and talents clearly.

The Dictionary defines 'self-awareness' as a person's clear perception of their personality, including strengths, weaknesses, thoughts, beliefs, motivation and emotions. It allows them to understand other people, how they perceive them, and their attitude and responses to them. I believe that purpose is often a reflection of strong self-awareness, and a lack of purpose a reflection of poor self-awareness. For this reason, this chapter is dedicated to nurturing self-awareness.

The more self-aware a young person is, the less likely they are to make decisions based on what they 'wish they were' or 'what someone else is doing' or for 'someone's approval'. A life that copies or mimics others is unsustainable and can only lead to unhappiness. For our children to find their path, they have to discover themselves.

Whilst I was teaching, I worked hard on developing self-awareness in my students as I believed it had a direct link to whether they reached their academic and extra-curricular goals. If they weren't self-aware, they wouldn't know when to ask questions, check for errors, reflect on their work or make connections while reading stories.

They also wouldn't know whether to give up, adjust or keeping pursuing a goal. A child who is self-aware will innately know whether to continue to follow dreams, and develop the necessary skills to reach goals, even in the face of setbacks. They will also know when to minimise effort in an area which they are unlikely to succeed in. For example, some children will not benefit from studying six hours each night in a subject area they have no innate talent in. They would be better placing their time and energy in areas of competence.

The Key is Exploration

Interestingly, self-awareness is discovered through looking both internally and externally. I would like to suggest that it is our job to expose our children to diverse activities, ideas, people, foods, cultures, sports, hobbies and art to help them make new discoveries.

I see too many parents pressure their children to commit to specialising early, sometimes in the name of discipline or even in an attempt to continue a family tradition or skill. A few children may have talents that require specialising at a young age, but most don't.

A child may try different activities and then decide he or she doesn't like them. This is normal. Even if your child excels at an activity, it is okay for them to lose interest in it. Children evolve and change quickly. Just because they chose an instrument at five years of age doesn't mean they will still enjoy it at ten. Of course, if your child is a chronic start-and-stopper, or gives up each time an interest requires commitment, you may approach this differently.

Fundamentally, I am suggesting that you be flexible. Try not to map out their life when they are only five years old! Importantly, tell your child that he or she needs to finish the activity as per their commitment to a season or school term before moving on. This shows children that they need to follow through, and not waste money.

I used to write a 'things we want to discover' list with my own children each school holidays. This included things like visiting music shops to look at different instruments, downloading film editing software and making movies, visiting new parks and walking tracks or going to Asian or Indian supermarkets to buy new food to cook with. It is easy to get into a rut as a family and not spend time on the unusual.

I am a big believer in play, acknowledging that the more we allow children to play, the more they experiment and discover themselves. A light bulb moment of mine was realising that the less I interfered with play, the more children learnt. I also found out pretty quickly that I couldn't discover a child's strengths for them; they had to make that discovery themselves. I could however, create an environment that highlighted and valued them.

Play offers children refreshment and is a therapy like no other. Children need as much of it as possible.

Big is Found in Little

Parents, I want to think of yourself as an explorer of your child.

Like any explorer, we need to pay close attention to the little things. Incidental words, actions and emotions paint a picture of who our children are. We need to be listening to what our children are telling us, not what we want to hear. It is easy to dismiss the things they talk about as unimportant, although they have the potential to provide us with insights about who they are becoming.

One big mistake that parents make is looking for big strengths that make their child stand out from others. It's easy to reward

Self-Awareness

exceptional talent, like being the smartest or the sportiest. The biggest or most visible talents are often falsely perceived as the best. In contrast, the smallest talents can produce big rewards for each child who uses them. Fully-developed small talents make big contributions to the world.

I always caution parents when I hear them disappointedly saying things like, 'All Johnny wants to do is go fishing.' I have a brother-in-law named Johnny whose sole interest in life was fishing. My mother-in-law realised very early on that there was something unique about his interest, so she never discouraged it even when it was at the detriment of his school work. Today he runs a very successful business, is regularly on television and is the fishing guru in his region. From our children's small interests, big things can develop.

You may be missing a valuable talent by underestimating the worth of their interests. Is the ability to daydream less important than the ability to do maths? I personally don't think so, as there have been many daydreamers who ended up as great philosophers. Is the ability to talk endlessly less important than the ability to play sport? No, let's not underestimate the power of sales and communication in our world. We need to be careful not to judge our children's strengths according to our biases or ambitions.

Notice what brings your child joy. While I subscribe to the idea that you can do anything, given enough time and effort, I don't subscribe to the idea that everything will bring you joy. I love to see young people embrace their differences, capitalise on their strengths and have the confidence to back themselves. My job as a parent is to allow enough space and opportunities for my children to pursue what brings them joy in life. Questions like 'How do you feel when …?' help young people connect action with emotional experience.

Asking the 4 WHATS

Failures illuminate our children's strengths and also their weaknesses. If we shelter them from failures, we rob them of opportunities to see themselves more clearly. Failing well demands we develop self-awareness to reflect and adjust future goals and dreams. There is no doubt that you learn more about who you are in the difficult times. Failure is an awesome teacher. It is a learning opportunity.

Michael Manos, PhD, has worked for more than 25 years in paediatric psychology, special education, and child and adolescent psychology. He suggests we start asking our children the '4 WHATS'. Although this strategy is used to help young people become aware of poor behaviour, I also believe the 4 WHATS is a great tool to boost their self-awareness after failures.

The first of the 4 WHAT questions is simply asking a child to identify the behaviour. 'What did you do?' is a great starting question. The second WHAT question deals with the consequences of the child's behaviour: 'What happened when you did that?' Connecting the dots between behaviour and consequences is a self-awareness skill that all children need. This link encourages a child's ability to see what effect their behaviour is having on the environment and people around them.

Once a child begins to understand the cause and effect connection, parents can then add the next two questions, which are related to future behaviour. 'What could you have done instead?' and 'What would have happened if you'd done that?' This predicting exercise helps young people learn and practise appropriate behaviour to replace inappropriate behaviour, or more effective ways to express themselves. The ability to predict human behaviour is strongly linked to self-awareness.

Using a Shared Journal

A shared journal is a beautiful way for children to explore themselves. For those who are naturally reflective or are gifted writers, shared journals are magical. In a shared journal a parent and a child take turns to continue a dialogue, sharing their thoughts back and forth and asking questions of each other. Some shared journals have themes that direct the conversation.

I notice that children who journal with a parent develop strong reflective skills. They are reassured of being responded to in a thoughtful way, which makes reflection more motivating to engage in. They also make discoveries about themselves that they may not make on their own. Imagine looking back on this journal as a young adult. I can't imagine a greater gift to give a child.

Here are some words from mums who have used shared journals with their children:

> Karen says, *I started the journal because I was surprised when my friend told me her 13-year-old daughter wouldn't tell her*

who her crush was ... and they have an excellent relationship! I was surprised by the first question my daughter asked in the journal ... it wasn't what I thought it would be, but I knew it was important to her. The journal means that if I'm busy, she can still 'talk' to me about important things. It's a good reminder to me that this age can be confusing with many questions and I would rather her ask me than Google it! Who knows what answers will pop up! My daughter is now 12 ½ years and just this morning, she said, 'This is an awkward and embarrassing question but ...' and she asked me straight out! Perhaps the book gave her confidence to ask me or trust that I will answer honestly and at her level. Either way, I love that she feels comfortable to talk to me!

Raylene, mother of triplets, says, *Yes, over the years we have done this with both our boys and girls. It can open the door enough for them to feel strong enough to say or share something they are feeling, or have done, seen or worried about. But can I say we have this agreement with our children: No matter what is written or said we will not react first; doesn't matter how unique it is, but listen. We also do it by leaving notes for them, even just reminding them we love them, are proud of them and even just thanking them.*

Danielle says, *I used one with my stepdaughter from ages eight to twelve. We both found it more comfortable to communicate our feelings this way for a certain period of our life.*

Jillian says, *My daughter and I have a journal where we write little letters, compliments and pictures. We love it.*

Self-Awareness

Melinda says, *I have used this with my son and it seems to work well. He doesn't use it quite as much as my daughter did though.*

Lisa says, *We don't have a journal as such, but we use little letters. My daughter writes a letter if she has any awkward or embarrassing questions then leaves it on my bedside table where I write one back and put it back on the bedside table. We started using it about two years ago when she was ten.*

Over the years I have encouraged parents to use it to discuss things that were tricky for them to bring up in person. One mum used it to talk to her son about her divorce. Another used it to discuss her daughter's friendship dramas. I have seen a shared journal be used by both mothers and fathers to support children who are self-harming, depressed or even ready to run away from home.

Another objective way to assist in developing self-awareness is through credible personality and psychometric tests, easily available on the internet. They have their place in discussing strengths, weaknesses, career ideas and relationship issues. These tools often appeal to children who are logical and may not enjoy the concept of a shared journal.

Choosing a Core Team

People who are self-aware continually compare their perception of themselves with other reliable sources. They don't just live in their own reality but ensure that reality is resonating with others. This sometimes requires asking hard questions.

One of my favourite quotes is, 'You are the only person in a room that you can't see.' Because of this I rely on a few trusted people to confirm or challenge my perceptions of myself. These people have proven their ability to tell me the truth as they see it. I have to realise I may not always be comfortable with their feedback, but it can be trusted.

It takes great self-awareness to reach out for help and lean on other people for perspective. Julie Harvey, head of Welfare at St James says, 'I have a few students who suffer from anxiety. They will come to my office and ask me if what they are thinking is rational. They are checking their perspective against my perspective. I greatly value this role in their lives. It takes self-awareness to recognise when you need to access others. It takes greater self-awareness to recognise who to access.'

Opening your life up to people's perspective is something we want to caution our children about. Too often I see children trust their peers in the same way they trust their family, with disastrous results. Young people need to know that their best friend will never treat them the same way that their mother does – nor can they be expected to. Friendships go pear-shaped when little ones overshare and believe that friends will be the same vault of support that they receive at home.

Similarly, young people can naïvely trust their social media friends. One girl I know recently posted an image of herself in hospital after a panic attack. At the time she hoped to shed light on the reality of anxiety and help others who were suffering. Unfortunately, her friends interpreted the post as attention seeking. I have seen young people trust a boyfriend not to share a nude photo, a friend not to forward a text or a private message – all of which is unrealistic given their age and maturity.

Well-meaning adults can also be guilty of insensitivity to children, offering opinions or implied advice inappropriately or unnecessarily. Many adults have recounted stories to me about their grandmother or aunty commenting on their body shape during puberty. We say things to children that we would never say to another adult. Inconsiderate labels and expectations can harm our children. Because their sense of self is still developing, children are particularly susceptible to people's critique of them.

I suggest that every parent be mindful of the words they use to describe their child. Welfare Officers often share their concerns about parents labelling their children. Harvey continues to share, saying, 'It's not uncommon for parents to come in and say, "He's got anxiety" even though they haven't been to a doctor or psychologists for a diagnosis. I find a lot of times their child is just "nervous" because exams are coming up. Anxiety is not the same as feeling nervous. I think a lot of kids started off being nervous, and they become anxious because of the labels and attention they were given at the time. I'd rather us not be so quick to self-diagnose.'

The role of trusted parents and support people is critical to help shape children's perceptions of their strengths and weaknesses and offer them additional insights.

Using the Trash

Children need to realise that not all feedback is worth internalising, but all feedback can help them define who they are, if they are able to think critically. Helping our children learn to process feedback well is critical. People's misdirected words can threaten to take us off course in life if we internalise them. This is why self-awareness is a brilliant resilience trait. Self-awareness enables us to listen internally rather than externally. It enables us to let go of negative words and hold to our own truth.

Talking through the validity of feedback will lead to one of two decisions: we either take it on board or trash it. I have often talked about 'binning' other people's ideas when I supported a teenager who was being harshly judged. We all need a special 'bin' just for people's unneeded and unhelpful opinions.

I see a lot of parents 'binning' negative feedback before their children have the opportunity to read it. Although this is sometimes essential, I caution parents about doing it too often. If we bin everything for them, they don't get the chance to learn to 'bin it' for themselves. Bin harsh words with them, not for them. Teach them to rip up the page and throw it in the trash. Words are powerful – but they are only as powerful as we allow them to be. Words often said in humour that are worth binning:

We all know you aren't the smart one. You are the sporty one.

Don't worry, we all put on weight as we get older.

I thought you'd be taller by now.

Good things come in small packages.

You'd look really nice with makeup on.

I am so proud when I see a young person fiercely protect themselves when their knowledge of themselves is harshly challenged by untrustworthy sources.

Self-Awareness

The challenge is not to allow people's opinions (to which we are more susceptible during dark times) to penetrate us so deeply that we compromise who we are. Once we know who we are, our job is to protect that knowledge.

Choosing What We Celebrate

Children compare themselves all the time – and that isn't always a bad thing. Comparisons can give us accurate perceptions of our strengths and weaknesses. For example, Natalie's friend Isabella was chosen for the state netball team. Natalie and Isabella used to play netball together. They were both on the same team and had the same level of talent. They were both good, but neither was great. Natalie got bored with the sport and dropped out, while Isabella continued, training three times a week and setting her sights on making the state team.

When Isabella announced that she had made the team Natalie was surprised, because she considered herself to have the same skill level as her friend. What she failed to recognise was that, through determination and hard work, Isabella's skill level had improved dramatically. This opened up a discussion between Natalie and her mum about talent, and the impact of effort on that talent.

When Isabella was celebrated at school, the teachers did a great job of celebrating Isabella's effort rather than her achievement. It is great to see teachers explain in detail and celebrate the effort behind achievements. In Isabella's case they said, 'Isabella gets up at six o'clock in the morning, and then goes back to training in the afternoon. She does that three times a week, even when she is tired. Last week all that effort paid off when she got into the state netball team.'

It's critical that we reward effort and not just achievement, as this builds accurate self-awareness. I'm all for giving rewards and singling children out who work hard. Real life rewards hard work applied to talent, and so should we. As Louise Klar, counsellor from Genesis Christian College says, 'The kid that wins has usually worked really hard. We don't need to take that away from him by giving everyone a participation certificate. Instead we need to explain why they are receiving the award and make each award meaningful.'

This can also be applied to discussions about our children's appearances. As beautiful or handsome as they are, they didn't earn their good looks. They were born with them. Unfortunately, children who are praised for things they haven't earnt don't always feel legitimately valued. Please, tell your children they are smart, courageous or strong, and don't put all their focus on their looks.

Some of the things that children receive awards for make me laugh. Almost every child has, at some point, received an award that holds little meaning. As a result, their certificate either sits in the bottom of their school bag or goes straight in the bin. I saw a child receive an award for getting a haircut once – a haircut! Another boy I knew got a 'player of the week' award when he wasn't even at the match! It seemed his coach had just set up a roster that automated awards each week.

Sometimes intrinsic recognition is enough. Knowing we are doing a good job, and having the self-awareness to recognise it,

Self-Awareness

is a reward in itself. The last thing we want is a child who melts down if they don't get recognised for their achievements. Self-awareness says, 'I know I did a good job. It is not the end of the world that I didn't get a ribbon.'

Take-home Tips:

- Be flexible. Try not to map out your child's life when they are only five years old!

- Write a 'things I want to discover' list with your child. We can help our children discover their life purpose by giving them the opportunity to explore their gifts and talents. Experimentation not specialisation is the key.

- Notice what brings your child joy.

- Remember that big is found in little. One mistake that parents make is looking for big strengths that make their child stand out from others. It's easy to reward exceptional talent, like being the smartest or the sportiest. The biggest or most visible talents are often falsely perceived as the best. In contrast, the smallest talents can produce big rewards for each child who uses them. Fully developed small talents make big contributions to the world.

- Play offers children refreshment and is a therapy like no other. Children need as much of it as possible.

- Be mindful about the words you use to describe your child, especially when they disappoint you. Words can be like labels which stick like glue.

- Help your child identify their core team. The role of trusted parents and support people is critical to help shape children's perceptions of their strengths and weaknesses.

- Help children identify who to share personal information with. Too often I see children trust their peers in the same

Self-Awareness

way they trust their family, with disastrous results. Young people need to know that their best friend will never treat them the same way that their mother does – nor can they be expected to.

- Don't place too much value on your child's appearance. As beautiful or handsome as they are, they didn't earn their good looks. They were born with them. Unfortunately, children who are praised for things they haven't earnt don't always feel legitimately valued. Real life rewards hard work and so should we.

- Teach your child to use the trash - but be careful to bin harsh words with them not for them. The challenge is not to allow people's opinions (to which we are more susceptible during dark times) to penetrate us so deeply that we compromise who we are. Once we know who we are, our job is to protect that knowledge.

One day your child will not only have to push through difficult times themselves, but they may have to shelter others, including your grandchildren. It takes strength of character to be fully responsible for one's time, actions, belongings, feelings and relationships.

5
RESPONSIBILITY
Find Your Own Way Home

My fifth year of school was a bit of a crazy one. My bestie got another bestie, which left me hanging as the third wheel. I wasn't connecting well with my teacher (who I had two years in a row!) and I was incredibly bored with the monotony of timetables and spelling. After school I would spend my time knitting jumpers, doing craft and starting little businesses. Between 3 and 9 p.m. I was in my element.

One day I decided that instead of playing hopscotch and elastics at lunchtime, I would jump the school fence and escape from my troubles for a while. I remember sneaking past the administration block, scrambling over a wire fence and then running for my life until I was around the corner and out of sight. This became my daily ritual, and I found myself daydreaming about my adventures during class. Sometimes I would visit elderly neighbours, pick flowers or hang out at the corner store. Looking back, I am surprised that no one at the school noticed!

At that time my father owned his own hairdressing salon. Every night he would bring home the float from the cash register. This made it really easy for me to fill my pocket with his coins. I sound like a really bad kid here, don't I?! Wagging school! Stealing! If you have a child who is wagging school or stealing your coins right now, be reassured, they just might turn out okay!

Dad's coins made my lunchtime adventure so much more exciting. I used to buy loads of 1c and 2c lollies and take them back to school with me. Sometimes I would have so many lollies left over that I would hide them in a neighbour's garden like secret treasure. I didn't want to take them home and be questioned over them. Anyway, with handfuls of lollies to distribute, I noticed an improvement in my social situation.

Responsibility

One day I convinced another girl in my class to join me on my adventure. It took me ages to convince her, as in Year 5 wagging school wasn't a cool thing to do. I had stolen money from my dad's change bag again, and I promised her all the lollies she could eat. Moments after the school bell had rung we made a run for it and arrived at the shops without getting caught. Needless to say, we had a great time!

While we were walking back to school, I noticed my dad's car driving towards us. I couldn't believe it. This had never happened before! I looked down – down as far as my head would go – but he had already spotted us. With little time to think, I quickly threw the Drumstick ice-cream I was eating into the kerb. Within seconds Dad had pulled the car up next to us and very graciously took the time to ask, 'What's going on girls?' I have no idea how I answered that question. All I can remember is that my heart was pounding!

My dad surprised me that day. Instead of giving us a warning (or a pep talk), he drove us back to school, marched us straight into the principal's office, and then left us there. He was as calm and collected as can be! The only words I heard him say were, 'Sir, I believe these girls were wagging school.' And then he literally turned around and exited.

I am sure that behind the scenes he called the principal and filled him in with a little more detail, but I didn't see that. My takeaway was: Dad's not going to rescue me. I am on my own with this one! Needless to say, I was horrified. I was honestly expecting him to bail me out! I was at least expecting him to wait outside of the principal's room to comfort me after I had gotten into trouble. But, no – he up and left.

I confessed everything to the principal, which lead to serious consequences! Back in those days the cane was the accepted method of punishment in schools. I got a few hard wacks to my rear end. I also had to give a series of apologies, which included standing in front of my whole class and saying sorry for leading them astray, buying them lollies and inviting them to wag school. I hadn't been in trouble before, so I smile when I think about what was going on inside of my head at that time. I remember thinking, 'So this is what it feels like to get into BIG trouble.'

A Mindset of Responsibility

Responsibility is the act of being accountable. We all know of adults who are unable to move past challenges because they refuse to take responsibility. They are constantly blaming, excusing and justifying why things can't improve, instead of being accountable for what is right in front of them. It is impossible to be resilient without being responsible. Without responsibility we become a 'victim'.

We want our children to take responsibility for their time, actions, belongings and relationships. We also want our children to take responsibility for their feelings. From a young age our children need to understand that they 'own' their feelings and it is their responsibility to manage and regulate them. As parents, we are undoubtedly here to help them but, ultimately, they have choices to make. Too often parents convey that it is their responsibility to 'fix' how their child feels.

Responsibility

There are many ways that parents unintentionally encourage irresponsibility. Some of these include:

- Justifying or excusing poor behaviour.
- Providing quick fixes to make children 'feel better'.
- Doing their homework and assignments for them.
- Communicating on their behalf.
- Giving them privileges regardless of whether they have earned them.
- Blaming others, including teachers or the school system.
- Not investing much time into teaching real life skills.
- Doing things for them that they are capable of doing themselves.
- Not giving them significant responsibilities around the house.
- Handing them money without any accountability being associated with it.
- Paying their bills.

The older our children get, the more responsibility falls on their shoulders. We have to remember that one day our children will not only have to push through difficult times themselves, but they may have to shelter others (including your grandchildren) at the same time. We know all too well the strength of character it takes to be fully responsible at both home and work.

Life is about options. Our choices are very powerful in creating our futures, and that is why our children need to feel the weight of them early in life. To become responsible with these choices, our children have to understand cause and effect. This can't happen if we bail them out, excuse their behaviour, give them endless supplies of cash or do everything for them. Responsibility can't be learnt when someone else takes our pressure for us.

I have often watched my children take responsibility on the sporting field, and was extremely grateful for the lessons they learnt there. If they didn't score a try or they dropped a catch, they could either give up and sulk, or take responsibility, refocus and keep going. I couldn't run on the field and sort it out for them. They had to make real-time decisions, and if they didn't quickly own up and 'move on', they would let the rest of the team down. If they are able to apply this same principal to every area of their life, I know they will be successful regardless of what life throws at them. This is resilience in action.

The Importance of Letting Go

Richard Branson recalls one day that he and his mum were out driving. He was apparently being a royal pain in the ass, which I can't possibly imagine! Let's just stop and appreciate the task this mum had on her hands. Can you imagine a 14-year-old Richard Branson telling you how to run your world? Anyway, in an attempt to teach her son a lesson, she abruptly pulled the car over and said, 'Get out and find your own way home.' Without looking back, she drove away. No bluffing there! She obviously assessed the risk, decided she would kill him before anything on the open market would, and made a calculated decision.

Responsibility

Instead of remembering that as a negative experience, Richard attributes it to his ability to do anything. Something clicked in him that day and he learnt that he could take responsibility for both his behaviour and finding his own way home. As I read Richard's story, I was reminded of how much our children learn from real-life experience. Words without actions fail to have the effect that we so often hope for.

It's the mindset of 'letting go' and letting life interact with our children that I want to emphasise, rather than dropping your son off in the middle of nowhere (regardless of how tempting that might sound)! We need to be prepared to 'let go' bit by bit – enough to allow them to learn. We have to be careful that we aren't so determined to give our children the best of everything, or the easiest path in life, that we over-protect them.

Experts agree that we are doing way too much for our children. I have often wondered if parents secretly fear that their children will be left behind if they aren't catered for. Maybe that is why we operate like a second brain for our children, who are always forgetting things like sports uniforms, assignments and lunches. I see parents pay their kids' bills, speak on their behalf, buy them excessive stuff and wrap them up in cotton wool, all because they fear that their children will fail.

One mum wrote to me saying, 'The hardest part is standing back and letting the boys do things themselves in their own time. They are so laid back. For example, organising schoolies, finding out where the formal is that he has been invited too, speaking to the teacher about assignment feedback. I would really prefer to know everything now and step in and take over and it takes all my might to sit back and go with the flow. When they come home from school I have so many questions and they just need to be left alone for half an hour. It kills me!' As a mum, I sympathise with her words. This is my house too!

When we let go, it's uncomfortable. We risk seeing our children fail. I have to regularly remind myself that I want my kids to make as many mistakes as they need to in order to learn. We have to be prepared to see our children fail in the 'micro', in order for them to win in the 'macro'. I notice a lot of parents aren't prepared to allow their child to fail because they feel there is too much at stake. However, while they are at home and there is a level of protection and safety, it is an ideal time for them to do that learning. The stakes are often much higher as they get older.

Thongs and Jumpers

I caught up with a mum over coffee this afternoon. She shared with me this gem, which is a great example of letting children build their own life from the ground up. She said, 'I don't want the first decision my kids make (independently) to be a life-changing one, like "should I get into the car with someone who has been drinking?" If they have never felt the consequences of little decisions they won't know how to make big decisions. That's why THEY choose whether they wear thongs to walk across a hot road or not. That's why THEY choose if they wear a jumper or not.'

It is uncomfortable watching anyone struggle, let alone your own children, who you have cared for since birth – so it takes commitment for parents to let go and let their children discover life. The reality of this style of parenting means that your teenagers will experience failures and things won't always be plain sailing.

Maybe your child is a dreamer and has grand ideas that you know have a high chance of failing. The temptation would be to block their ambition. Maybe he or she wants to try out for a sporting team that you know they won't get picked for. The temptation would be to talk him or her out of it. Maybe your child struggles with anxiety and instead of trusting teachers at school to care for them, the temptation is to be on speed dial, ready to bring them anything they request.

The temptation is to fill in all the gaps in our children's lives so they don't need to stretch themselves by asking for help, solving problems or taking risks. By stepping back, we give our children confidence that they can't gain any other way. We say to them loud and clear that we have confidence in them and their ability to get through challenges. We hand them their lives to take responsibility for. Their life is a gift.

It's *their* gift – not *ours*.

Calculating the Risk

One of a parent's main roles is to protect their child. We're not just talking about a child's physical safety, but emotional and social safety as well. There is often tension between protecting a child and allowing them to make mistakes or fail. Resilient children grow up to calculate risk well because they have practised making mistakes. During these times they have had opportunities to assess their capabilities and their limitations, and their tolerance for the gap between the two.

With each year their children grow, parents face the challenge of letting go a little more. I distinctly remember feeling the drive to protect my boys from taking risks when they were learning to surf. The waves they wanted to surf and the waves I thought were safe to surf were two totally different things. I wasn't sure they were assessing their capabilities accurately.

After surfing for some time (and not drowning), my eldest got his license, so the two of them were able to go up the coast and take those risks without my supervision. The tension I felt when they had 'gone surfing' was real! Were they wearing sunscreen? Were they keeping an eye out for each other? Were they checking for rips? I am sure they came home with amplified stories about nearly crashing into rocks and drowning just to wind me up!

Despite my inner turmoil, I realise it was good for my children to have healthy ways to push boundaries and challenge themselves. The risks our children want to take may seem silly in our eyes, but they are developing their stories and strength. Whether it be to try out for a lead in a school musical or start a small business or participate in an action sport, we have to let go enough for them to pursue their dreams. The pursuit of healthy purpose leads them to discover resilience.

Parents have many questions about the appropriate age to give children independence. As these parents wrote:

At what age do I let him ride his bike to his friend's house? It is about a five-minute bike ride.

I used to walk to school every day but for some reason I am scared to allow her to do it. It seems crazy to be so concerned about her getting kidnapped by a random, but I am.

Responsibility

When is the best age to let them go to the shopping centre or movies by themselves? I will be there the whole time and they have a mobile phone if they need me urgently.

It's difficult for parents to calculate the real risk a child faces and determine what to protect them from and what to release them to discover. That's why we often turn to our mothers for advice – but in this case, Grandma might not be the best person to ask. As people age, they naturally get more cautious.

After reading the above statements back to the parents who wrote them, most started laughing at how over-protective they sounded. Wayne said, 'At their age I would leave the house for hours at a time, no mobile phone, and my parents didn't even know where I was playing. I seemed to survive as a child without 24/7 supervision, but these days it's different.'

As with all risks, education and preparation are essential. There is nothing like a little risk management from a parent along the way. I am not suggesting blindly saying 'yes' to a child without helping them understand the consequences of poor or miscalculated choices. I also caution parents about being too relaxed about technology. It is the only area in which I feel we underplay the potential danger.

Children need us to get out of the way so they can discover their own capabilities. Without a parent to turn to for support, our children need to solve problems and make decisions on a whole different level. There are some risks that children won't take when a parent is watching over them, so the parent's absence is actually essential. Similarly, there are some mistakes children won't make if their parent is on the sideline cautioning them.

Here is some advice that your children will love me giving you:

- If the physical risk is minor (to medium), let them go for it.
- If you are concerned for their reputation and they aren't, let them go for it.
- If you think it's a silly or pointless idea but they don't, let them go for it.
- If you usually watch them at ballet every week, try doing the groceries instead.
- If you always pick them up from school on time, try being five minutes late.
- If you call them three times a day, stop it.

Research confirms that resilience is only built through exposure. So let's let our kids discover life before their desire to is squashed.

Trusting Teachers

I see parents' inability to let go and trust teachers and the school system as one of our biggest barriers to building resilience in children. On the whole I believe teachers get a bad rap. They are far more perceptive and much better at their jobs than many parents give them credit for. Unfortunately, parents are often quick to defend their children without asking adequate questions or gaining more information. It backfires on our children as they get the impression that authority can always be challenged, questioned and disrespected. It gives them an opt out, when they need to be opting in!

Responsibility

Peter's teacher rang his mum, as Peter's assignment had not been handed in on time. His mum could have made a lot of excuses for him or even tried to get him out of trouble. That is what this teacher was expecting, so he rang a little defensively. He had already phoned three boys' homes and each mum told him the same story, 'He is going through a rough patch right now', or 'I'm so sorry. I'll be more vigilant to get on to him in the future.' Behind the phone line, this teacher was rolling his eyes.

This mum's reaction was refreshing. She said to the teacher, 'I completely agree with you. He's been irresponsible. Give him a detention. Give him two or whatever you see fit.' When Peter got home that afternoon he was astounded that his mum hadn't defended him. She had thrown him under the bus! Mum simply said to him, 'Are you Superman? Yes, you are to me and I adore you. Are you above the law? No. I am not going to rescue you from your poor choices. I love you too much and you are more than capable.' I LOVE this mum's response!

Minimise the Incident

I spoke to Chas Gullo, father of four, about the mistakes his children made when they were young and how he handled them. He talked to me about the difference between expected behaviour and appropriate behaviour. I loved this because it highlighted the mistakes young people will inevitably make as they bridge the gap between the two. 'Helping them take responsibility shouldn't be about conflict with our kids,' Chas explains. 'I used every conflict as a position of education. I have never seen conflict as a negative. It becomes a practice for peace making. Peace making is a gift.'

Chas continues to explain, 'One strategy I used was minimising the incident in order for them to own their mistakes. Just say a neighbour's window was broken because they were throwing rocks. If I needed to ask, 'Who threw the rocks?' and got no response I would then say, 'Who threw the *small* rocks?' He found that if he minimised the incident someone's hand would be more likely to go up. This shows me how difficult it is for children to take responsibility for their mistakes. Our reassurance of that ownership is important.

Chas also cautioned against nagging and pleading with children to do their chores. He suggested that parents correlate each important responsibility to a privilege, that can only be earnt by independently completing that responsibility. This way parents can more easily leave it up to their children to decide when and how they should get that task done.

Although it's not always possible to make that correlation, we can be conscious of doing it when we can. Some things that parents might say include:

- Once you have cleaned up your room you can play.
- Once you have unpacked the dishwasher I will take you to your mate's house.
- Once I see your homework is done then you can get your phone.
- Eat your vegies and then you can have dessert.

Responsibility

Teaching Life Skills

Sue writes to me, saying, 'I believe that contributing around the house is important, but it is such hard work! She put two dishes in the dishwasher tonight and I am going to praise her about that, because that is as good as it is getting at the moment. She has no concept of the world beyond her. They only have energy for themselves. They don't think they have any capacity, but they do. How do I get that capacity out of them?'

Children gain competence, self-reliance and more empathy for others through simply doing household chores. There are so many benefits from having children do chores that we can't afford to dismiss them as worthless. Research suggests that children who do chores from a young age (three or four years old), are easier to engage in chores as a teenager. They are also more likely to see a need and fill it when it comes to the real world if they do so at home. Chores help them gain skills that last them a lifetime.

I believe that too often we give our children chores that are menial tasks like putting their laundry in the basket. However, our children need to feel their contributions are legitimately needed – not in lip service, but in real tangible ways. Household chores need to stretch children, not bore them. I encourage you to pick a task that is challenging for them and teach them how to do it.

The general rule is, don't do things for them that they can do for themselves. This includes packing lunches, cleaning, washing and doing assignments. It's less convenient and it takes longer to teach our children how to do real-life tasks for themselves, but in the end the reward will be worth it. The potential risk of letting them do their own washing is that they will shrink something, or it won't be dry when they need it. It's a small risk in the scope of life, and a risk that we are best incurring while they are young.

There is a difference between giving a child a token job and a legitimate job. If tasks are a stretch for their age, they are legitimately learning something from the experience. Sometimes parents need to be honest and say, 'I have been treating you less capable that you actually are.' Try giving them more responsibility, rather than less, and see if they rise to it.

I thought this was a great insight from Karen, mother of four, who talked to me about cleaning the house like it was a team sport! She said, 'You have to be a role model. When parents start cleaning, children are more likely to be involved. It says, "This is the direction that we are going in the family, and I need you to come along."'

The Importance of Creativity

'Temporarily improving your child's immediate mood will not allow them to undertake actions to produce longer term effective change,' states Dr Judith Locke, author of *The Bonsai Child*. Please, let them be bored. If they experience the pain of boredom, they also experience the pleasure of creativity. They have to be bored in order to work out how to create and solve problems. Without the low they don't get the high.

I have seen parents go to ridiculous lengths, buying their children excessive things or pandering to their every need, all for the sake of keeping the household peaceful and happy. Parents are usually well motivated, but at the end of the day their children

Responsibility

need to be able to be resourceful and creative when they feel down or negative. Remember, we ultimately want them to take care of their wellbeing.

It also has to be said that a child's online life has the potential to squash creativity because it rules out options. There are heaps of creative things you can do with an iPhone, but there are also many that you can't do. Having screen-free time is essential so our children don't lose contact with other ways to be creative.

Using creativity is one of our children's great responsibilities in life. It is through creativity that our children express themselves to the world and interact with others.

The hardest part about creating is making a start. Once our children start, they receive a surge in dopamine, a naturally-occurring chemical associated with reward and pleasure. This helps them feel happy and motivated to keep going. Many school holidays I remember helping my kids get started building a cubby house ... and then I left them to it.

I Don't Know, Try

There is a big link between confidence and responsibility, but few directly make this link. When I see young people refusing to take responsibility, they are usually struggling to believe they can handle it. Their attitude may come across as over-confident, cocky, lazy or rebellious, but I find that a lack of responsibility is usually based in self-doubt.

I especially see this when young people leave Year 12 directionless. They may throw caution to the wind because internally they have given up; they fear not measuring up or being enough. They aren't yet confident enough to trust their own journey without comparing themselves with everyone else.

You may notice that your children deeply question themselves during challenging times. Questioning is not a bad thing, but it is how these questions are answered that makes all the difference. A loss of a friend, a bad mark at school, struggling health or even a separated family can cause our children to doubt themselves. What they think and do during these times is so critical to their future. Questions enable us to discover ourselves.

I listen to children and teens who get stuck in a world of 'I can't', 'I'm lost', 'I don't want to', and hear myself in their complaints. Children express their fears much more transparently than adults. Over time we learn to accept and even embrace our fears. It is only through repeatedly having to face challenges that we learn that we do have the strength to get through them. It may be helpful to remind ourselves that this is our children's first rodeo! They haven't yet learnt that the tide comes in and out.

When self-doubt is plaguing a child, our reassurance can make a big difference. However, there is nothing like being able to answer the nagging questions of doubt for yourself. Sometimes the only way for young people to find the answers they are looking for is to have a go. As the saying goes, 'If you try you might fail. You guarantee failure if you don't try.'

I have said to my own children, 'I believe you can, but you have to find out for yourself.' Having a go is the only way you will really know. Am I good enough to make the netball team? I don't know – try. Will I pass that exam? Let's see. If I ask that girl out, will she say yes? Only one way to find out!

Responsibility

It's easy to answer self-doubt with inflated praise or hypothetical answers, but it is more effective to answer it with action. Recalling previous times when they have handled pressure may give them perspective. 'I don't think I can do this,' they might say. 'Remember when you did ...,' is a great way to reply. Children don't trust someone who criticises them all the time, but neither do they trust someone who praises them all the time.

Be careful of not inflating your praise. Let your feedback be grounded in fact rather than fluff.

Take-home Tips:

- Parent with the future in mind. We have to remember that one day our children will not only have to push through difficult times themselves, but they may have to shelter others (including your grandchildren) at the same time. We know all too well the strength of character it takes to be fully responsible at both home and work.

- Let your child learn from real-life experience. Words without actions fail to have the effect that we so often hope for. We have to be careful that we aren't so determined to give our children the best of everything, or the easiest path in life, that we over-protect them.

- Reinforce that life is about options. Our choices are very powerful in creating our futures, and that is why our children need to feel the weight of them early in life.

- Don't give your child technology every time they are bored! Using creativity is one of our children's great responsibilities in life. It is through creativity that our children express themselves to the world and interact with others.

- When possible, correlate each important responsibility to a privilege.

- Realise that as parents (especially mums!) we tend to over-calculate risk and under-calculate the reward. Next time your child asks you for autonomy, ask yourself, 'What's the worst thing that can happen?'

Responsibility

- Don't do things for them that they can do for themselves. That includes packing lunches, paying for things, cleaning, washing and doing assignments.
- Trust teachers more.
- See yourself as more than a gap filler. The temptation is to fill in all the gaps in our children's lives, so they don't need to stretch themselves by asking for help, solving problems or taking risks. By stepping back, we give our children confidence that they can't gain any other way.
- Be careful of inflating praise. Children don't trust someone who criticises them all the time, but neither do they trust someone who praises them all the time. Let your feedback be grounded in fact rather than fluff.

A misconception is that self-care is about pampering or making yourself feel better, when it is actually quite a very different concept. Self-care enables us to be strong – mentally, emotionally, physically and spiritually – so we can give to others.

6
SELF-CARE
Watch Out For Geckos

Self-care isn't something that I have connected with easily. In theory I understand the importance. However, in practice I find myself resistant to adjusting my schedule to allow time for self-care. When my life is already full, self-care tips – like moisturise your body every night – make me do a massive eye roll!

The thing that I have struggled with the most is finding what self-care strategies work for me. I hate massages, and getting my nails done amongst a cloud of toxic fumes doesn't excite me. It's taken me a little while to be able to answer the question: what replenishes and energises me? Self-care is an individual journey.

At the heart of self-care is ensuring you give the best of who you are to people and tasks, while not living in a depleted state. Self-care can help you enhance your health and wellbeing, manage your stress and maintain productivity. A misconception is that self-care is about pampering or making yourself feel better, when it is actually quite the opposite. Self-care is the acceptance that I have to take responsibility to be strong mentally, emotionally, physically and spiritually, so I can give to others.

As I have expanded my view of self-care, it has become more inclusive of where and how I invest my personal energy. It has become about committing to those things that are uncomfortable for the sake of building a stronger person for the future. This might mean stopping comparing yourself to others, walking away from gossip and taking more time to make important decisions. These things do me more good than a facial! This doesn't mean that the occasional self-indulgence is wrong, but regularly indulging in activities or purchases that are not affordable in the name of self-care isn't something that benefits *me*.

I had to find things that I was already doing and add intentionality to them. I was already walking, so I adjusted the time of day I was doing it so it also enabled me time to reflect. I love cooking, so I intentionally used it as time to take care of my body. I love people, so I spent more time in positive social environments. Interior design, the water and beautiful environments relax me, so I indulged a little more in those things.

I have also learnt to be more flexible and listen to my body. Some days I rip up my to-do list and discipline myself to rest. That doesn't mean I don't apply myself on every other day, but some days I just need to replenish myself. When my body and mind is not strong, I don't produce my best. I have also had to monitor my perception of stress, and not overreact to things that are irrelevant in the big picture. It takes determination to focus on the things that matter.

We are all unique. We are also evolving as people, and the self-care methods that worked for us last year may need to be adjusted this year. I have had to be prepared to experiment with self-care to discover what works and what doesn't work. Much like a baby tasting food for the first time, I can't tell if I like something if I am not prepared to try it. With practice and attention to it, I can honestly say that self-care has become something I value greatly.

The Difference Between Teens and Adults

The word self-care emphasises personal responsibility. It's not called parent-care or friend-care for a reason. Knowing how to self-care is a skill that can take anyone a long time to learn.

Even grown adults look for someone else to comfort and rescue them! Why? It takes self-perception to find strategies that truly work, especially because we are always growing and evolving as human beings.

In my book *Parenting Teenage Girls in the Age of a New Normal*, I discussed the difference between how a young person and an adult may implement self-care strategies. How we self-care changes according to the stage of life that we are in. Self-care for a two-year-old is very different to self-care for a 12-year-old and a 30-year-old. Renegotiating what your self-care looks like in each stage of your life requires a reassessment of what is working and what is not working. Self-care requires you look at your entire life to discover what you need next. It takes foresight.

Because young people are prone to looking externally instead of internally, they often copy the self-care strategies of others. They may look at what the reality TV stars do or what their friends do. I find that young people's 'down time' is often spent wishing they were someone else or somewhere else, instead of truly nurturing themselves and being honest about who they are and what fills them with joy.

During puberty young people are experimenting with new ways to self-care. As parents, we have to be flexible in allowing this to happen. We might offer them the same self-care strategies that worked when they were younger, such as staying home to rest or going out as a family. Unfortunately, what worked then won't necessarily work now. We can be working with the old game book even when young people have written several updated editions.

Long periods of time in their bedroom can be a normal part of self-discovery, as may be a frequent desire to socialise. Remember also that dictated methods of self-care seldom work. Self-care strategies work because they bring reward or perceived reward.

In saying all that, I see great value in our young people participating in self-care strategies that they may not currently use. Families may deliberately work self-care into their family's daily routine for everyone's benefit. For example: setting aside time to talk, cooking healthy food together or exercising together. Adding self-care strategies into a family routine enables young people to broaden their self-care skills and adopt strategies that may be different from their own. Research suggests that eating together as a family improves teen's grades and psychological health – even when the teen says they are not getting along with their parents.

Self-Care Strategies

I like to encourage children to choose ten self-care strategies and display them somewhere visible. That way, they can easily refer to them. These strategies should be a combination of things they can do by themselves and with others. The reality is that people aren't always available when we would like them to be, so having a mix of strategies is practical.

Here are some strategies children might like to experiment with:

- Have a conversation with someone you love.
- Read a good book.
- Make something.

- Organise your room.
- Paint or draw.
- Write in a journal.
- Compose some music.
- Put makeup on or style your hair.
- Take a warm bath or shower.
- Put on comfortable clothes.
- Wear different textured socks .
- Drink hot milk.
- Cuddle a teddy bear or blanket.
- Put on perfume or light a scented candle.
- Watch your favourite online show.
- Think about happy things.
- Finish your homework or assignments.
- Help someone.
- Be helpful around the house
- Cook (or help cook) something healthy to eat.
- Watch funny YouTube videos
- Play with a pet.
- Do something that moves your body, like stretching, swimming, running, dancing or riding your scooter.
- Squeeze something like a stress ball or plasticine.

Self-Care

The Mind Body Connection

Escaping real life to spend time online can seem like self-care. Unfortunately, it often only complicates social stressors, disrupts sleep and replaces physical activity. Primary school principals and teachers are constantly telling me that they wish parents would help children put away their phones in the hours after they get home from school. This way children have time to reflect and process their day without their peer's interference. If conflict has arisen, they are able to step back before they respond. It's like a circuit breaker that prevents their system from overloading.

Marianne Connolly, Director of Junior School, St Paul's School, Bald Hills, comments, 'I only get to hear about issues when they are going badly. I would prefer they didn't get to that point. Many of the issues I see could be avoided if children have less phone time straight after school. They need to have the opportunity to talk about those things they have experienced and reflect on them, before responding. Issues just continue, usually on a downward spiral, without the opportunity to reflect. It's amazing how much it impacts their learning.'

Whenever I have worked with a young person who is struggling with resilience, my ideal starting point is to see them take better care of their physical body, which often means a little less screen time. They are always reluctant to do this, so slowly, step by step, I hope to be able to show them the benefits. If I can strengthen their body, it automatically strengthens their mind. I have found the mind—body connection very powerful in my work.

There is conclusive evidence that health is enhanced by physical activity. It is recommended that children and teenagers

(5 to 17 years old) accumulate a minimum of 60 minutes of moderate to vigorous activity each day. However, 80% of 13- to 15-year-olds world-wide do not get this amount – so if you are reading this and you have a non-sporty child, they are definitely not alone!

An association between physical activity and mental health has also been reported in one study in the *Journal of Adolescents*. One of the most interesting findings was that those who were least active were at much higher risk of anxiety and depression compared to moderately and highly active adolescents. Bottom line: if we can keep young people moving moderately, it may be enough to support them.

Not surprisingly, there were also increased benefits for those depressed, anxious or experiencing suicidal thoughts if they participated in team sports. It was concluded that participation in sport offered benefits over and above the actual physical activity alone. I knew a young person who had enrolled in lawn bowls and loved it! I don't think it is the intensity of the activity that gives our children benefits, but the commitment to regular moderate movement and the community that encompasses it.

Finding Reward in the Right Place

I recently spoke to some Year 11 students about gaming and the reward system which attracts them. We also talked about habitual and voluntary behaviour to help them understand how important early prevention and intervention is when it comes to any addiction. This is discussed more in my book, *Self-Harm:*

Self-Care

Why Teens Do It and How Parents Can Help. This information is critical to get into the hands of young people.

Gaming addiction is something that concerns many parents. I have often listened as parents have described their children's behaviour when they have limited the amount of time they are allowed to spend on gaming. Their children become angry, irritable and unable to regulate their emotions. Young people don't always regulate the 'sensibility' of their actions, so they struggle to make reasonable judgements.

You can get addicted to anything that has a reward attached to it. Gaming is all about easy rewards – but there are better rewards. When you are gaming you don't have to deal with chores, family issues, friendship dramas, anxiety or school work. You get a hit of dopamine quickly and easily. You may get a sense of control, entertainment, identity and a feeling of competence.

Connolly goes on to talk about the impact she sees on children who are excessively gaming, 'We can tell kids who do a lot of gaming simply by their mood and behaviour at school. We deal with some students who are gaming for six hours a day on the weekend. After the weekend their mood is terrible. They can't concentrate, are aggressive, negative and uninterested in participating. You can see they haven't exercised, and they are fidgety. As the week progresses, they slowly come out of the fog that has surrounded them.

'Children who play before school often have arguments about technology with their parents in the morning. They simply don't want to get off once they get on. If it has been a bad morning at home, they come into the classroom unfocussed and difficult to engage. They are still thinking about the game that their mother told them to put down, so they could get ready for school.'

Another primary teacher recently told me a story of a usually alert and sporty boy in Year 6 who became lifeless and tired almost overnight. He was setting his alarm and waking up at midnight, and then playing games through the night. His teachers could see that something wasn't right. He wasn't himself. Poor mum nearly died when she found out. It's astounding how strong a pull gaming can be for our children. I am constantly hearing reports from parents about how difficult it is to say no and how 'left out' their children feel if they are not online, even in Year 4.

It takes courage (for both us and our children) to say 'no' to easy rewards and help our children embrace better ones. When parents put in the effort to help their kids experience rewards from healthy places, I believe they give their children a huge head start in life. Face-to-face relationships, enjoying the outdoors and accomplishing goals are all real-life rewards.

Real life is the best reward.

Misplaced Energy

Everyone's energy is finite. Where our children place their energy impacts their mental health.

Teenagers are typical for misplacing energy, and not having the self-control to focus on what is good and healthy for them. They can easily spend their night worrying about what someone thinks of them, even if they have an assignment due the next day. They can easily lose sleep over someone else's friendship drama. This is valuable time they could be using to self-care!

Self-Care

I asked a group of teenagers about where young people misplace their energy. When they all simultaneously answered 'friendship dramas' I asked them to give me a specific example. 'All of high school,' they laughed. One of the boys piped up and said, 'It's pretty easy to avoid really. All you have to do is have no friends.' This whole conversation made me laugh, as I remember the drama associated with high school all too well. One fight between girls in my year level and I didn't hear another word the maths teacher said.

Young people often define a friend as one who will emotionally support them, but this support can come at a huge price to them personally. Empathetic distress is a term used to define the stress caused by internalising the perceived suffering of another person. Research has recognised its impact on academic performance and the quality of peer relationships. Interestingly enough, empathetic joy is equated with more positive friendships and school experiences.

It's important that we spot signs of empathetic distress in our children and consistently redirect them to self-care during these times. We also need to talk to our children about what a good friendship looks like, as part of their understanding of self-care. These discussions can help young people create an understanding of where to invest their social energy.

These are some qualities great friends have:

- They don't need drama to enjoy their day.
- They have a respect for your study and sleep time.
- They respect their own study and sleep time!
- They don't ask you to be their counsellor, mother or babysitter.

- They don't just want to talk about problems.
- They enjoy your company.
- You feel stronger around them.

Watch Out For Geckos

One of my neighbours has a security alarm that goes off multiple times a day. It's so annoying (for them just as much as me!), especially when they are at work and they can't turn the alarm off. It keeps going and going and going all day long! Apparently, some security alarms are over-sensitive. They can get set off if there's a burglar breaking into the house OR if there's a little creature (like a gecko) walking in front of them.

Children have a personal security alarm inside of their brain. When their brain perceives a threat, their personal security alarm goes off. That makes their heart pound faster, and their feet want to run really quickly. An alarm is designed to get us moving away from threat as quickly a possible. Our body's fight or flight system is based on the perception of approaching stress. Sometimes our personal alarm is set off by something legitimately life threatening like a burglar. But more often than not (just like at my neighbour's house) it is set off by something small, like a gecko.

It takes time for our children to learn to let the geckos pass by their alarm system without reacting to them. When little things happen in our children's lives, it can create a lot of unnecessary stress until they learn how to categorise it as insignificant.

Self-Care

Something as simple as not getting their own way may seem like the end of the world rather than a manageable hick-up on the road of life.

One of ways that young people can self-care is monitoring their perception of stress. Different stressors can be perceived as challenging or threatening in various degrees of intensity. Perception categorises stress as bad stress or good stress. Good stress is perceived as 'challenges that can be overcome'. Bad stress is classified as 'overwhelming' and disrupts the normal function of the brain and related systems.

Stress has a far-reaching impact, affecting young people's quality of life, so the management of it isn't something we want to be too casual about. It is important that our children do everything they can to engage with it only when necessary. If our children jump to the worst-case scenario all the time, they will unnecessarily live in a state of fear that will exhaust their bodies and minds and render them unable to enjoy life.

Part of growing up is developing a mindset that says, 'I have control over how I perceive life and how I respond to stress'. However, remember that young people have the potential to label everything as life threatening because their inexperience doesn't give them perspective. Their physical responses to everyday stress may be largely the same as when their life is in danger.

So, the question I ask young people is: how great a threat is this, really? Is this the end of the world, or a part of the obstacle course? Questions like, 'How much time and energy do you want to invest into this?', 'Will this be important in five years' time?', 'How long do you think it will take to blow over?' might help them gain this perspective.

Signs of Stress

During challenging times, when stress levels are high, our bodies rely on our ability to recalibrate to regain balance. This balance is called homeostasis. If your body does not recover from stress it can suffer harmful effects. For those who experience trauma, a lack of recalibration can lead to long-term and lasting mental health problems. This is where self-care and resilience connect. A child's resilience is boosted when self-care strategies are used to manage stress.

If our children live in a depleted state, they are more likely to struggle during their next challenge. Much like a marathon runner, they need to be in peak condition to complete the race. A depleted physical state will only make them more likely to injure themselves or fatigue too early. We never know what tomorrow is going to bring – for us or our kids. So, keeping our family healthy gives them a good starting point if they need to respond to a crisis.

We can be on the lookout for signs that our children's reserves are depleting. Small changes like going to bed later than normal or numbing out in front of a screen are things worth noting. A child's lack of joy concerns me. When children stop smiling, laughing and being curious about the world, I am prompted to ask questions.

Stress affects your entire body. You may have a child that gets a headache every time exams are on, or a child who refuses to go to sleep because they aren't 'tired'. We all have individual responses to stress. We need to understand that stress affects each individual differently, and therefore the list of signs below is not comprehensive:

Self-Care

- Headaches.
- Loss of appetite.
- Stomach aches.
- Low energy.
- Muscle tension.
- Increased irritability.
- Difficulty concentrating.
- Negative self-talk.
- Changes in socialising.
- Frequent colds.
- Acting out.
- Waking up in the night.
- Having trouble falling asleep.
- Changes in online habits.
- Wanting to remain busy all the time.
- Crying.
- Being more dependent.
- Bedwetting.
- Nail biting.
- Withdrawing.
- Being perfectionistic.
- Talking less and becoming more withdrawn.

Don't Belittle Feelings

One mistake that parents make when trying to bring perspective is belittling young people's feelings. What may be a tiny stress in your eyes could be huge in theirs. Meeting a child where they are at is one of the great arts of teaching. To teach our children how to handle stressful times, we need to be prepared to look into their world and experience what they are experiencing.

Here are a list of things which Year 6 students told me 'rocked their world'. I was surprised how small many of these things were.

Losing one shoe in the morning.

Breaking something at home.

A running race.

Dropping my books or lunchbox at school in the middle of the port racks.

Friday spelling tests.

Being the slowest in the class.

Forgetting something.

Not getting to pick my clothes.

Words like, 'It's not so bad', 'You shouldn't be worried about that', 'You have nothing to worry about,' may seem helpful in your eyes, but actually tell them their feelings aren't valid. When we do this, we run the risk of shutting our children down. We don't want our children to suppress stress. This is a really important point for us to understand. If children suppress their feelings, they go inwards.

We want our children to express rather than suppress emotions. Words that encourage them to express themselves may sound like, 'I can see this is upsetting you,' 'Would you like to talk about it?' This gives them an opportunity to *both* express their emotion and adjust their perspective.

Stress Hacks

Stress can be really helpful, so we don't want to spend our life trying to avoid it. In moderation it can boost our immunity and make us more alert and responsive. However, our children do need to learn to manage it.

Watching a young person have a panic attack is just horrible. Parents who have children who experience panic or extreme anxiety can help their children by teaching them how to respond to it. In the process, they will increase their sense of control and wellbeing.

When children feel anxious and they enter a noisy classroom, things can escalate really quickly if they don't have a plan of action. If a person next to them is being distracting, they may want to move but may be reluctant to in case they are considered 'mean' or 'unfriendly'. Moving is not mean. Rudely telling your friend off for being distracting might be mean. Talking about him or her to others might be mean … but moving is not mean. Moving is just looking after yourself. It is important that friends allow each other to look after themselves without judging them.

Finally, I would suggest that a student tries to have a chat to the teacher, after class or during a more appropriate time, to explain how the noise in the classroom can make them feel. Hopefully they can come to agreements to either modify the acceptable noise level or change their seating position. I have even negotiated with schools to allow their students to remove themselves during a lesson without asking, or to walk around at the back of the room if they feel restless.

Researchers are continually finding new and simple ways for young people to control panic. These usually rely on a young person's ability to recognise it quickly and take action in order to activate different brain networks to calm things down. These are a list of suggested actions when a young person's fight or flight system is activated:

- Recognise what is happening.
- Breathe deeply, from your diaphragm (so underrated!).
- Describe three things you see around you.
- Touch three things that are close to you.

Take-home Tips:

- Teach the real meaning of self-care – the acceptance that I have to take responsibility to be strong mentally, emotionally, physically and spiritually, so I can give to others.

- Talk to you child about the most valuable types of self-care which may include stopping comparing themselves to others, walking away from gossip and taking more time to make important decisions.

- Realise a young person's self-care strategies will be different than a child or adults. During adolescents they are experimenting with self-care strategies that work for them.

- Watch for signs of stress. A child's lack of joy concerns me. When children stop smiling, laughing and being curious about the world, I am prompted to ask questions.

- Recognise your child's individual response to stress. You may have a child that gets a headache every time exams are on, or a child who refuses to go to sleep because they aren't 'tired'.

- Ask your child to identify ten self-care activities that don't involve a screen, and then try one or two before you picking up their phone or playing a video game.

- Encourage your child to do something that energises their body every day.

- Realise that technology detoxes are essential if we want our children to identify the impact that technology has on them. I encourage young people who are struggling with self-care to unplug from technology for the day, weekend or even week.

- You can get addicted to anything that has a reward attached to it. Gaming is all about easy rewards – but there are better rewards. Take the time to explore things that give your children better rewards.

- Encourage your children to express rather than suppress emotions. Words that encourage them to express themselves may sound like, 'I can see this is upsetting you,' 'Would you like to talk about it?' This gives them an opportunity to both express their emotion and adjust their perspective.

Self-Care

The day I said to myself, 'Not on my watch', I identified that I had a 'watch' or a responsibility to contribute my gifts and talents to other people. We all do, including our children.

7
CONTRIBUTION
Not On My Watch

I was 17 years old. It was my first year of university and I was studying teaching. My friends and I were enjoying weekends at the beach like most kids our age who live in Queensland, Australia. I was also involved in running a Friday night youth program, which sometimes operated from skate parks. This gave me plenty of opportunity to help people young people, which was my purpose and passion.

A girl called Skye arrived at our program one night. Skye was about 13 years old, but she looked as if she was about eight. She was excruciatingly thin and small in stature, yet with an older woman's face. I was later told that she had suffered extreme abuse as a young child and that her normal physical development had been delayed through ill mental and physical health.

That was enough for me to be concerned for her wellbeing and future, and I believed that somehow our lives had crossed for a reason. I made it my mission to take extra special care of her. I offered to pick her up in my car each week so she could attend the program consistently. I knew it was the highlight of her week. She was always dressed and waiting for me when I arrived. I can't remember being concerned about the cost of petrol, or feeling she was a burden on my schedule or time. I enjoyed seeing her smile.

Skye lived with her mother and little brother. I can only guess he was about four years old because he hadn't started school yet. I soon noticed that every time Skye left the house, her little brother would cry in distress (no – scream in distress!). I didn't have any knowledge about trauma or attachment theory, but I knew that this little one needed his big sister. So, I did what made sense to me. I put him (and his car seat) in my car.

Contribution

I will always remember the relief in Skye's eyes as we bundled him into the car each week. It was like she needed him too. She would carry him around on her hip all night and he would patiently rest there. Skye was the main caregiver to him, responsible for feeding and bathing him. They were very close.

The more I spent time with her little brother, the more I noticed how quiet he was. I often tried to talk to him, but got very little response. Others would also try and interact with him, but we never heard him say a word. When I asked Skye about this, she simply said, 'He can't talk yet.'

I can't describe what happened in my heart at that moment. This 'soon to be' teacher responded with compassion in bucket loads! I remember saying to myself: *No. Not on my watch. This kid is going to talk!* This makes me laugh so hard now, because I was all of 17, and had no idea about the complex needs I was trying to deal with. All I knew is that I wanted to make a difference and I saw an opportunity.

In the weeks to come I arrived earlier than normal so I could tutor this little man (haha). I brought picture books and alphabet letter games with me, and lollies and gold stars for rewards. At first, the poor kid was so scared of my enthusiasm he didn't even want to sit next to me, but slowly, slowly he and I became mates. Slowly, slowly ... he began to talk to me. His first sounds were muffled noises rather than words, but I heard sound! That was all I needed to hear.

I can't tell you the reward I felt in that moment. I had tears, his mum had tears, everyone who I told had tears. In my mind I had conquered the highest mountain, and all with one desire to make a difference. I had proven that compassion could lead me to exciting and fulfilling places. I knew from that moment on that it wasn't a degree that would make an extraordinary teacher. It was heart.

What caused me to give up my time and petrol money (not just once but on a weekly basis) as 17 year old? I felt I could make a difference. It was the same thing that drives me in my career every day. The day I said to myself, *Not on my watch*, I identified that I had a 'watch' or a responsibility to contribute my gifts and talents to other people. We all do. Our children also do.

Being Needed

Contributing means making a gift or payment to a common fund or collection. When we contribute we put our hat in the ring, along with many others, to make people's lives better. There is no one person who can change the world, but collectively our contributions make a big difference to others.

Our children, although young, contribute their gifts to the world every day. They have endless ways they give of themselves – a kind word, a smile, a helping hand, an invitation or a word of encouragement. School, home, sports teams and part-time jobs provide opportunities for young people to make contributions. I always remind my children that it is one thing to notice a homeless person or a need in the community, but it is an entirely different thing to allow those same observations to move you to action. Actions are what define contribution.

When young people contribute, it makes them feel like a necessary part of this world. If their contribution is required consistently, it will demand that they keep going in spite of challenging personal circumstances. This is how contribution interacts with resilience. Contribution gives each of us a reason to keep going in the face of pain and discomfort.

How many times have we heard parents say the thing that enabled them to get up in the morning during a difficult time was their children. The fact that their children relied on them strengthened them to continue. When others need us, we know we will be missed if we are absent and we have a big reason to keep going. The truth is that sometimes it is easier to do things for others that we wouldn't do for ourselves. The motivation to contribute to others is a significant and important driver that can't be underestimated in maintaining resilience.

Islands of Competence

To make a meaningful contribution I believe there has to be a certain intentionality about it; therefore children have to develop an understanding of who they are and what skills and traits they have to offer. Competence, or the ability to do something successfully or efficiently, has a lot to do with the contribution a person can make. The greater developed the skill or talent, the more intentional we can be with it.

Dr Robert Brooks devised the term 'island of competence' to describe a child's unique strengths. He writes, 'Islands of competence were not intended simply as a fanciful image but rather as a symbol of hope and respect, a reminder that all individuals have unique strengths and courage.'

Developing a young person's strengths is critical to enable them to have the courage to develop greatest competence in areas they find challenging. Doing something well shifts one's sense of self. Dr Brooks writes, 'If we can find and reinforce these areas of strength, we can create a powerful "ripple effect" in which children and adults may be more willing to venture forth and confront situations that have been problematic.'

Many children do not feel academically competent, and adopt self-perceived inadequacy. The shame associated with going to learning support is a real one for many. We've created a narrow schooling system in which children are tested against others and have limited opportunity to discover their own islands of competence. If a child is able to genuinely say, 'I do have an island of competence – it's just not in maths', they have a powerful reminder of their uniqueness. This confidence can be a life saver for children who excel in arts, sports, social ventures, business, etc.

It's interesting how we prepare young people for a lifetime of contribution by competition. By the time young people are at the end of their school life, competition is unfortunately deeply entrenched in them. Comparisons, performance indicators and benchmarks fill our school system and reinforce the message, 'I get ahead by being the best.' However, marvellous teachers (of which there are many) can play a big role in helping young people compete against themselves rather than others.

I don't think that our children hear often enough that they are loved the way they are. I encourage parents to enjoy their children just the way they are – without fixing them or demanding they mature. Parents need to say, 'I value you. I accept you. I enjoy you. I am proud of you. I love you and you don't have to compete to get my attention.'

Contribution

Whenever I meet with parents, teachers, or other professionals, I ask them to describe a young person's strengths. Next, and importantly, I ask how these strengths are able to be displayed for others to see. In other words: how can their child contribute their strengths so they are visible, and in their visibility are reinforced. This strengths-based approach is my go-to time and time again. It can work at home, school or work.

The Contribution of Humour

The ability to laugh at yourself and with others is a beautiful gift in life that we need to make sure we nurture and enjoy. Many of our young people have a special gift in this area. One of my sons particularly lights up my life with his banter. Likeability is a huge head start in life. Seeing the funny side of life helps us cope when things don't go our way. Humour is protective. I love this quote by G.K. Chesterton: 'Angels can fly because they take themselves lightly.'

Stepping into humour during tense times diffuses challenges. It bonds people together and it creates memories and stories that we tell time and time again. One lovely idea is to keep a journal of all the funny things that your kids do and experience. We so easily forget the good times when things get tough. I have a few memories written down, but I wish I had started this practice earlier.

When my youngest son Matthew was about four years old, he often played with a mate across the road who was the same age. We lived in a cul-de-sac, so they used to run between each other's houses. Anyway, one afternoon, when I was dead tired and asleep on the couch, the two of them had a fight.

As the story goes, Matt thought he saw his friend steal something from our house. The rest of the details are a blur, but I know things escalated very quickly. I awoke to a lot of screaming (blood-curdling screaming!). In a panic I ran to my front door to see my son chasing his mate up the street in a rage, with a hammer in his hand. Obviously, his fist had not done the job, so he had gone into the garage to get a hammer to seal the deal. NO ONE was going to steal from his family.

At the time it wasn't funny. Several neighbours had come out to see what all the commotion was about, and I was sure my son was going to forever be labelled Rambo. I felt bad for leaving them unattended. I felt even worse knowing his mate was freaking out and in a mild panic. Apologies were made, and the whole thing took a few hours to settle. The next day they were playing as usual – which is the absolute joy of boys' short-term memory.

In the coming days his mate's mum and I started seeing the funny side of things (thank God she didn't hate my son forever!). It became something we started talking and laughing about at the dinner table with Matt, who began also to see how silly it must have looked and how scared his mate would have been. To this day Matt is reminded to 'take his hammer out' if someone threatens our family.

I tell you all that to say this: humorous family stories are the thread that bind us together. Dad jokes, repeated one-liners and quirky mannerisms all provide opportunities for humour. The older our children get, the more important it is for them to learn to use humour to diffuse tension and see another perspective. Humour is often a life saver on the playground.

Don't Be a Drama Llama

Positively contributing to a group is each child's responsibility. That requires our children to know how to handle gossip well. Gossip is another name for passing on mean information that might be unkind or untrue. Many young ones struggle to identify what is gossip and what it isn't. When is it okay to debrief with a friend and when does it cross the line? Conversations can start off healthy and change pace very quickly.

I find myself using the old-fashioned game, Chinese whispers, to explain gossip. When information is passed from person to person it is amazing how it changes and becomes distorted. That is why people say it is best to mind your own business and not repeat information that you overhear, especially when it is something ugly or mean. That includes well-meaning young ones who choose to be the messenger of bad news, telling friends that they have overheard someone speaking meanly about them.

When someone hears gossip, it usually triggers an uncomfortable feeling within them. That feeling should be a warning sign for our children. Gossip feels more like a game than a conversation. So once our children identify gossip, what do they do? Wisdom gives the person being mean an opportunity to self-correct. Let me explain how this may play out.

The truth is that children aren't teachers or parents. They don't have authority over their friends and – bottom line – it is not their job to tell them off. This is a really important point for children to understand.

The good news is that gossip dies through neglect. If children don't play the game, there is no game to play. Stepping away from gossip is the only way to really make sure mean words don't stay alive. Imagine a circle, where a group are playing Chinese whispers. What if one person in the group just flat out refused to play? The game is over.

On the first instance of being invited into a mean conversation, I would recommend young people try a distraction technique. Perhaps softly say, 'Hey I wouldn't worry about it', 'Let's talk about something fun', 'Have you seen this funny YouTube video?' Moving the conversation on usually is enough to tell the other person where you stand. Always try to say 'no' to someone gently first so they have the opportunity to self-correct.

If that doesn't work and mean comments are repetitive, you might have to talk to them more directly by saying, 'I'd rather not talk about Sarah.' Notice that this statement doesn't make a judgement about the other person. It's not, 'I don't like how you always gossip about Sarah.'

Ultimately, if that doesn't work, you'd have to ask yourself if this is the right group for you. It might be best to move on out of there! This may be easier said than done. However, the truth is that if gossip is intentional and consistent, at some point it will be targeted at you. Choosing friends that know how to self-correct is vital! This quote from Karen Salmansohn, summarises what every young person needs to know - 'Be a no drama llama. Don't create it. Don't invite it. Don't associate with it.'

You might also like to talk to your child about two times when mean information needs to be passed on. The first time is when children overhear something that is illegal or potentially dangerous (which won't be very often!). In these cases, an adult in authority needs to be told straight away. For example, if they overhear someone talking about robbing a house.

The second time is when a child hears something that genuinely upsets them. In this case, they need a 'Mr or Mrs Nobody' who they can talk to. That could be a mum or dad, grandma or aunty, or even a youth pastor, sports coach or boss at work. It needs to be someone that doesn't pass on the information, unless it needs to be taken to authorities.

Everyone is tempted to play the gossip game from time to time. Children might be particularly tempted to if it makes them look powerful or important. However, helping our children place value on their gut feelings is something that we can encourage. Gossip might look and feel good in the moment but, just like sweets, it doesn't nourish us.

We need to continually help our children know how to solve problems positively, cautioning them about involving others in their dilemmas. For example, asking a friend how to deal with the situation or involving a peer to help them sort it out! This is when civil war breaks out! Another big caution is getting involved with gossip online. This is when international war breaks out!!

Offsetting Weaknesses

My greatest joy has often been talking to boys about offsetting their weaknesses within a school setting. I just love their honesty about their struggles with teachers and organising their school work. This is Kane's story, which I hope helps you understand how it's important for young people to be aware of their strengths and know how to capitalise on them.

Kane was a typical impulsive, happy-go-lucky boy trapped in a private school that expected more self-control than he was able to muster. He was really well liked by his peers and had strong interpersonal skills. He had been described but not diagnosed as ADHD. He was definitely unorganised. He lacked interest in schoolwork and learning.

Kane admitted to being bone lazy. He rarely did his assignments on time, and when they were done, they were done poorly. He was a nice kid but a teacher's nightmare. He was annoying the heck out of the school! Kane was 'on contract', which meant that he had a list of things he had to stop doing in order to avoid a suspension:

- No calling out in class.
- No hands on others policy.
- No social media for six months because he had posted an inappropriate comment about a teacher.

One Tuesday he and two of his mates were in the art room finishing their assignment. It involved the use of ink which, by the end of the lesson, was all over their hands. The teacher asked them to go to the bathrooms to wash their hands thoroughly, and to remember not to touch anything on the way. So the three of them, hands in air, started making the journey across the school to the boys' toilets.

On the way to the bathrooms the boys saw a soccer ball lying on the ground. On autopilot and not considering the implications, all three of them started racing towards the ball. Forgetting the ink of their hands, Kane put his hand on the shoulder of his mate who had reached the ball first. Result: a mate with a big, bold ink handprint on his shoulder. Kane had done it again. Ignored a critical instruction from a teacher.

Contribution

Although he apologised, the school wasn't so forgiving. They were tired of Kane not paying attention to details and being a larrikin. Kane had no idea what the big deal was. It's just a shirt, he thought. 'Just replace the shirt. I'll get money out of my own bank account and buy him another shirt,' he insisted. Problem solved.

But the school wanted a bit more from Kane. They wanted him to listen, pay attention, respect their requests and stop clowning around. When mum and dad came to see me, they were at their wits' end, trying to fit Kane into a school context that he had no regard for.

I had to break the news to mum (and the school) that, regardless of their best efforts, many things about Kane would never change. So often we talk to boys like Kane about what they are supposed to do. They have a list of things to STOP – which, if we are honest, is not likely to happen. Instead, I always write a list of things they can DO in order to offset their weaknesses and contribute to an environment in a positive way.

I wrote a can-do, offset list with Kane which read:

- As you leave the classroom, thank your teacher for teaching you.
- Make eye contact with your teacher as you walk in the room.
- Play some type of sport for the school.
- Ask at least one question about school work in every lesson.
- Tell your teacher when you have started an assignment.

Teaching our children to contribute and make an effort is critical, then teaching them to make that effort *seen* and *known* is the next step. I call this 'offsetting'. I challenge young ones to contribute more than they are taking away from a classroom or work environment! If Kane does learn to offset, most teachers will put up with him calling out every now and then.

So, bottom line: we need to talk to our children about what to do and not just what not to do.

The World Our Children Will Create

Resilience has a lot to do with not deflecting accountability for who we are and what we contribute to the world. I have to *own* my talents and I have to *be responsible* for them. I equally need to own my weaknesses and their impact on the world. Being able to monitor and hold yourself accountable for behaviour is important. Young people who aren't accountable can grow up to deflect, blame, give excuses for not contributing.

I believe that contribution is found in our character. You can have all the talent in the world, and not have the character to contribute to the world or sustain that contribution. There are so many highly-talented and gifted people in the world who have committed suicide or lost their life to drugs because their character wasn't developed – only their talent.

Our children will live in a world that is created and led by those who contribute. Inventions, philosophies, ideas and movements will change our world as we know it. One of the little people I speak to in my presentations is sure to do something groundbreaking in the years to come and I will say, 'I knew them!' I remind myself of this every time I address an audience of little people. They are thinkers and dreamers. The contributions they make will come out of the hearts and minds.

Fostering Volunteering

We need to foster contribution in our children. What experiences could you give your children that would broaden their understanding of the world, and how they might contribute to it? Many of those experiences are offered within school, but what about outside of school?

The lifestyle we create as a family either provides room to volunteer in the broader community or leaves this important opportunity untapped. Little things like stopping to take an old person's trolley back to the trolley bay, being on the tuckshop duty roster, putting your hand up for sports coaching or working bees, or spending time talking to a neighbour going through a hard time are manageable ways we can volunteer our time.

It can be genuinely hard to get children to volunteer, especially if what is required is outside of their current interests or skill set or in an unfamiliar or uncomfortable setting. Research suggests that the younger we start volunteering as a family, the easier it will be for children to accept. Research also confirms that young people are more likely to volunteer if they have a best friend volunteering, and are more likely to consistently volunteer if their family volunteers.

Everyday Resilience

Here are some ideas based on what other families are doing:

My eldest helps me coach a primary school hockey team.

We, as a family, volunteer at our church, and at a supply centre for missions.

We all help out with a charity close to our heart. Student leadership at school. Peer support.

Helping with out-of-school activities such as fairs/events.

As a family we are very active volunteers with our baseball club. Our boys help out at working bees, serve in the canteen, assist at training with the younger players and umpiring games.

Volunteers with the local PCYC (Police-Citizens Youth Club).

Leads a primary girls aged group once a month.

Dog washing/drying and crate cleaning at local dog rescue.

English tutor with St Vinnies Charity.

We do up Christmas hampers at the local community centre. Volunteer at park run. Nursing home visits too.

Paddy's Van run by St Patrick's College. Offers food and a chat to the homeless.

I work at a not for profit so my kids will often come with me on school holidays.

Scouts has a service component, so mine learnt to volunteer this way.

School coffee cart.

Surf lifesaving and beach patrols.

Now that my daughter is a freshman, she volunteers at her old grade school by assisting her coach with her old cheerleading team. She also volunteers at the food pantry a few times a year.

I volunteer with a dog rescue. Something I started doing to give me something to do on the weekends the kids were with their dad. Now they come with me and we also foster! At 14 and 16 years old, they love teaching the younger kids about rescue and how to treat dogs.

Our daughter volunteers with Girl Scouts. We feed meals at a local church, put out flags at the cemetery on holidays, donate to the elderly and disabled ... and so much more

The Girl Who Changed My Life

In my very first year of establishing Youth Excel, I met Ashlyn. At that time I was delivering small group programs for local high school – girls at risk of dropping out of education. Each of these programs had room for eight students, handpicked by the guidance officer. The Girls Excel program aimed to improve school attendance and each girl's ability to cope with the challenges they were facing. I had six months to teach them resilience.

Ashlyn was one of about 80 students in my weekly programs. Out of all the girls I have encountered over the years, I remember Ashlyn the most clearly. Ashlyn's family was unlike mine, and many of her experiences were quite foreign to me. Her childhood was full of things she tried to put behind her: the absence of a father, physical abuse linked to her mother's poor mental health, alcohol addiction, and the intervention of the Department of Child Safety. She experienced sadness, isolation and instability in levels that no child should have to experience.

One of the most obvious differences between the two of us was our photograph collection. I literally had an entire cupboard full of photos of my childhood (yes, my mother was a bit camera happy and still is!). It was a built-in cupboard that housed album after album of images of my birthdays, overseas holidays and private school education. Ashlyn had a single photo of herself as a young child.

At her age I had few cares, if you don't count which boy I liked or whether I was allowed out on the weekend. On Ashlyn's 13th birthday she was setting up home in the garage of some older friends who were her temporary carers. It was no wonder that Ashlyn had been hand chosen by her school to attend my program. She fit the criteria perfectly.

Before too long Ashlyn and I developed a special bond. Each week Ashlyn would make her way down to the school fence and wait for my little red car to arrive. She would madly wave to me as I arrived in the school car park. Now, admittedly, I wasn't the only reason she was waiting by the school gate – she would always slip in a few smokes while she was there – but, in any case, I knew I was an awaited figure in her life. I got the sense that even five minutes alone with me was something she looked forward to.

On the way from the car to the classroom, Ashlyn would fill me in on her week. The highlight of her week usually involved any progress she was making towards finding her father. You see,

Contribution

Ashlyn had spent the last two years working with a government agency to locate the father she had never met. And she had a fantasy that one day he would be the saviour of her situation. He would be the missing piece that would make her life finally make sense.

It was during the course of my program that she got a phone call from the department to say they had finally tracked him down. But, unfortunately, Ashlyn's father refused to speak to her or have anything to do with her. Full of anger and rejection, her mental health problems escalated and her life hit rock bottom. Her hope of having a family was shattered. It was this hope that she had hung onto through every painful moment of the last 15 years. In her opinion, having even one loving parent would have changed everything. She was right.

Ashlyn was surrounded by teenagers who were complaining about how horrible their mothers were and how over-involved their parents were in their lives. 'Big problems!' Ashlyn would respond. She was surrounded by peers who were jealous of her freedom and ability to be independent, but she had maturity beyond her years. She knew better.

Over the next few months Ashlyn clung to me at the end of our sessions. There were times when I found it hard to let her go. Thoughts of Ashlyn would often fill my mind on the way home from work. How could parents just decide to disappear? I tried to hold my judgement back with the same determination as I tried to hold my tears.

I remember the day that Ashlyn snuck up by my side at the end of class and quietly asked me for some money. As I questioned her about why she needed money, I could feel her anxiety rising.

I asked her when she had last eaten. 'A few days ago,' she quietly responded. 'I'm not a big eater.' I couldn't help but wonder how, with a whole canteen full of food available, not a morsel had found its way to this child over the last few days.

That day, on the way home, I realised one thing. Ashlyn wasn't asking me for money. Ashlyn was asking me if I would do what her parents couldn't or wouldn't do. She had asked me if I would be the one to fill the gaps in her life. That day I made a decision to respond in the best way I could. There are plenty of Ashlyns who need us to be someone of significance in their lives.

Over the next few weeks I introduced Ashlyn to a few positive social programs. In conjunction with the guidance counsellor, I helped her with a tutor and some new subject choices. I organised mentoring, so she had someone to call after hours when she was feeling overwhelmed and needed to talk. I carried change in my pocket each week and bought her a salad sandwich and chocolate milk from the tuckshop.

The school would thank me for how much I was doing to help Ashlyn, but what they didn't realise was how much Ashlyn was doing to help me. Ashlyn changed my understanding of the difference I could make in young lives. She taught me that hope and love are easily transferred and life changing to those who receive them. When we give, it is given to us.

When we believe we are truly making a difference, we will do everything in our power to continue to make that difference. Just because we are going through a hard time doesn't mean we should pull back and stop contributing, although there are occasions when time and energy restrict our contribution. *Giving* often gives back to us at a greater rate than we can give out.

Contribution

Take-home Tips:

- Help your child become aware of their 'watch' and the vital contribution they make as little humans.

- If you want volunteering to be a part of your child's life, start as early as possible. The lifestyle we create as a family either provides room to volunteer in the broader community or leaves this important opportunity untapped.

- Create an offset list with your child. Expand the conversation. Talk to your child about what 'to do' rather than what 'not to do'.

- Find your children's islands of competence. Developing a young person's strengths is critical to enable them to have the courage to develop greatest competence in areas they find challenging.

- Remember that children watch how you contribute to society. Little things like stopping to take an old person's trolley back to the trolley bay, being on the tuckshop duty roster, putting your hand up for sports coaching or working bees, or spending time talking to a neighbour going through a hard time are manageable ways we can volunteer our time.

- Help your child step away from meanness. The good news is that gossip dies through neglect. If children don't play the game, there is no game to play.

- Smile, laugh and tell dad jokes. Humorous family stories are the thread that bind us together.

- Remember that contribution gives each of us a reason to keep going in the face of pain and discomfort. Just because we are going through a hard time doesn't mean we should pull back and stop contributing, although there are occasions when time and energy restrict our contribution.
- Note to self: *Giving* often gives back to us at a greater rate than we can give out.

Contribution

―――

Contribution gives each of us a reason to keep going in the face of pain and discomfort.

―――

It takes resilience to walk through the discomfort of parenting, but that is exactly what we need to do: keep walking.

Celebrating Resilience

I recently attended my son's Year 12 graduation where I looked around the room and pondered the different challenges children had experienced throughout their school years. For some children, chronic illness and other momentous losses compounded the already turbulent time of adolescence. For others, social difficulties or academic challenges had been a daily battle. Every child's challenges, regardless of their severity, shaped them in unique ways and played a significant part in their growth.

I am sure that every parent, at some point, has wondered if their child would make it through their lowest moments. During times of frustration parents have often asked me, 'How do kids learn this resilience stuff anyway? I am not sure what I am doing is getting through!' I always reassure them that children learn through 'seeing and doing'. By modelling and emphasising what matters every day, they are more likely to 'see and do' consistently.

The Mirror System is an interesting discovery which points to how children's resilience traits are acquired. Mirroring is when a brain's 'mirror system' fires in synchrony with the other person's movements, causing a simultaneous reaction in our own bodies. An example of this is when someone yawns, you have an uncontrollable urge to yawn as well; or when someone injures themselves you find yourself recoiling in pain.

Although there is lot of research that still needs to be done, we can assume that seeing and doing branch off the same 'tree' and there are many social behaviours learnt through observation, mimicking or copying. It is suggested that mirroring might be the mechanism by which empathy, gratitude, courage, and perseverance is learnt. Interestingly, there has also been a connection between dysfunctional mirror regions and social disorders such as autism.

Mirror neurons were first discovered in the 1990s when researchers found that individual neurons in monkeys' brains fired when they grabbed an object and also when they watched someone else grab an object. Researches haven't been able to prove that humans have distinct mirror neurons like monkeys, but they have proven that they have a more general mirror system.

Research has also identified differences between mirror neurons in monkeys and the human mirror system. At the early age of 18 months old we can regulate our imitation. That means we are able to perform the action differently from the person we are imitating. What makes us different than monkeys is that human beings can regulate what they mirror. Simply put, our children have a choice.

Research suggests that we are more likely to mirror people whom we trust and identify with, as mirroring shows a willingness and openness to understand someone and genuinely connect with them. For this reason, mirroring often occurs in family units or amongst close friends with whom we have spent a lot of time. Infants primarily gather their social skills from their parents.

Internal states, such as desire also impact what and how we mirror. Just because you see something doesn't mean you will automatically mirror it. Learnt behaviour is complex. A young person's genetic make-up and reward system comes into play.

You may have heard the saying, 'You are the sum of the five closest friends that you have.' If you want to be more grateful, courageous, positive, you are best to surround yourself with people who have those characteristics. If you want your child to be all those things, the first step is practising them in your own life.

Next time our child walks through the front door with the words, 'I hate school', 'I can't do maths' or 'I have no friends', remember the mirror effect. In the future they may find themselves doing, saying and being as they have seen us do, say and be. Remember too that young people do what they are rewarded for, so they need to see and feel benefit from their actions.

The Resilience Workshop

Over the last 20 years of my career, I have seen young people develop resilience by simply, yet intentionally, putting one foot in front of the other. In even the most severe cases, long-term triumph is found in the small choices that children make every day. Every time a young person who hates school gets dressed in the morning, they are strengthening resilience. Every time a young person speaks their mind, asks a question in class, shares their dreams or tries out for a sports team after they have failed, they strengthen resilience. I can't emphasise enough that daily decisions *matter*. Resilience is a by-product of exercising the traits we have talked about in this book.

However, as a parent myself, I am conscious that my children may grow up without the urgent need to exercise traits of resilience. Courage, gratitude, empathy, self-awareness, responsibility, self-care and contribution are traits that are often drawn out of us through necessity. Without the benefit of hindsight, our children may not fully realise how critical each of their small choices are. Like most of our younger selves, quick fixes and instant results are far more attractive. That is why conversations about resilience, and associated daily choices, are so important.

The daily grind of helping children prioritise resilience can be exhausting, frustrating and draining. If you have listened to the dilemmas of friendship drama or academic pressure for longer than 20 minutes this week you will know what I mean! I call these 'revolving door' conversations, because they seem to go around and around with no end in sight.

If your child is experiencing a problem they can't solve or a circumstance they feel stuck or unable to make progress in, I want to alert you to the fact that you are right in the middle of coaching resilience, so be patient. It's easy to miss the value of the monotonous, time consuming, repetitive conversations we have with our children. Many of these conversations are backdropped by the same pressures that we may remember experiencing at their age.

I liken parenting to being a resilience coach. Each time we deliberately engage in conversations which coach resilience we are inviting our children into the 'workshop' where resilience is conceptualised and outworked. The title of resilience coach can be tough to live up to sometimes, but in the words of Edna from The Incredibles, 'Done well parenting is a heroic act.'

Reflecting with Young Adults

I recently listened to a twenty-year-old reflect on her adolescent years and how her resilience was built through exposure to challenges. Rachael thoughtfully explained, 'I had leukemia and chemo twice when I was young. Once when I was 7 and once when I was 13. The second time I had it, I think it was easier to deal with. I knew I had gotten through it before. I guess it increased my resilience to being sick. The first time around I hated needles and the second time I was like, "Blah no problem," I built up a tolerance for hospitals and people treating me like a sick kid.'

Rachael came to recognise that exposure can develop resilience. Interestingly, she also went on to explain, 'I also think it affected me in another way. Because I wasn't at school for a few of my middle school years I didn't get exposed to much of what happened at high school. I didn't build up resilience to gossip or people being mean. I wasn't used to being rejected. I ended up a really shy teenager as I had always lived in an adult world. I was used to people taking special care of me.'

These statements are so insightful. I hope all our children will one day be able to reflect with such maturity. For me, these insights reinforce why our children need to fully experience life's challenges. Our job is to put our faith in them rather than the pain surrounding them. By doing this we give them a supportive environment to grow. Believing in our children wholeheartedly allows us to 'let go' and focus on supporting their potential.

In the section below I would like to continue to share young adults' reflections on their high school years. I love talking to this age group as they are young enough to remember and old enough to think critically. As they reflected, these young adults realised how their 'gritty' stories made them stronger.

As you read these statements you may think of your own child. Reminding ourselves of times our children have exercised courage, gratitude, self-awareness, empathy, self-care, responsibility and contribution can help us appreciate their steady progress. I hope you enjoy these reflections as much as I did.

Courage

Caleb, aged 18 says, *I was new to Oz tag and got pretty good at it quickly. I wanted to try out for the state Oz tag team, but I was told that I had little chance, as the team from the previous year were all planning to try out again. I decided to turn up, push through nerves and try out anyway. I was too nervous to play my best and felt like I collapsed under pressure. I didn't make the team, but it took guts to try out and people noticed. I did try out the next year and got in.*

Danni, aged 20, says, *I hated Year 8 compulsory dance class. I can't dance let alone dance in front of people! Part of the end-of-year assessment required me to create a three-minute interpretive dance and perform it in front of the class — solo! I contemplated wagging the class, chucking a sickie or refusing to participate, but instead I chose to dance. I passed the assessment with a C- and a few chuckles from my classmates. Then I chose to drop 'dance class' for Year 9. At the time I thought my performance would be disastrous, but it taught me that I could get through embarrassing things.*

Gratitude

Gavin, aged 24 says, *My parents had just split up. I was really aware of the financial pressure on mum. It made me appreciate everything we had a lot more whereas before I just took it for granted. I had to grow up quickly and do my bit. It made me stronger.*

Melony, aged 19 says, *All my friends had all their formal paid for by their parents. My parents were going through a financially tough time and couldn't afford to pay for everything. I felt like I was the odd one out. They paid for half of my dress, but I had to pay for makeup and my hair to be done. I remember making a decision to not make a big deal about it. Looking back it was a big growing up time for me and I felt proud of myself that I could work hard to earn my own money.*

Empathy

Chloe, 19, says, *I struggled through a lot of challenges as a teenager. My parents fostered and then that ended badly, with him [the foster child] treating me in a way that was inappropriate. Now my sister is really struggling with anxiety. Because I have already been through it, I can help her. I guess that is what exposure to something does. You get strong enough to help others.*

Tim, aged 18, says, *I became known as someone who would help other people, especially kids with anxiety who would get bullied. It was part of what I was known for. I got a sense of confidence from being helpful and I always knew that people would return the favour if I ever needed it.*

Self-Awareness

Kayla, 22, says, *I was about 14 when I started to notice that I didn't like going out as much as others my age. When I was asked to three parties on the weekend, my stomach felt sick at the thought of socialising that much. I just preferred my own company. After 10 p.m. I turned into a pumpkin and didn't cope well the next day if I didn't sleep. I am still the same today, and I think I always will be. I function better as a person if I don't compare myself to others.*

Michael, 21, says, *I remember the first time I talked to dad about something that was serious in my world. I was so embarrassed. Everyone in the house had noticed there was something wrong with me, but I kept shrugging them off. Then I followed dad downstairs and after about half hour I got the courage to talk. Once I talked to dad, it was much easier next time. It made a big difference to be able to trust someone.*

Responsibility

Sarah, 19 says, *If it was raining and there was a chance that netball would be cancelled, I would always turn up just in case I was needed. My coach would always meet me with a smile as she recognised that I was committed.*

David, 22, says, *When I was 14, I was at a party with my friends, which I was told would be supervised by parents. About an hour into the party my friend's parents left, leaving supervision to an older sibling. The older sibling invited her friends over, and* soon there were drugs and alcohol everywhere. *Things were getting messy pretty quickly, as more and more people turned up. I quietly slipped out the back door, walked to the street corner and called my parents to pick me up.*

Self-Care

Siobhan, 18, says, *My dad actually wanted a boy so I always felt like he didn't love me. Growing up, I worked harder than I should have for his acceptance and to prove to him that I was good enough. My dad's acceptance isn't such a big deal to me now. I've built a tolerance for his negative words and ideas. People who did accept me slowly became much more important for me. I focused on their opinion of me. The two people who made me feel accepted were my grandmother and Poppi. I was also pushed into finding belonging from people outside of my family, and these people became more like my real family. In the long run it hasn't been a bad thing for me.*

Ben, 20 says, *When I know I have an exam the next day, I get myself ready for bed early. I never did this in high school, but I find it saves me so much stress in the morning. Instead of finishing watching the movie that the rest of the family are watching, I'll go and sort my lunch and get some quiet.*

Contribution

Grant, 17, says, *I have always been the clown of the family. When dad comes home a little tense, I know I can help lighten the mood by cracking a few jokes. When dad cracks a smile – my work is done.*

Michelle, 18, says, *When I was in Year 7 I set a goal to raise $200 for an orphanage that the school was sponsoring. I came up with a plan to sell chocolates each Monday and Wednesday after school, and asked neighbours to take boxes of chocolates to work with them. That really made me feel like I wasn't just a kid but could do something worthwhile.*

Concluding Thoughts

As you have read this book, I have no doubt you would have considered your child's resilience level. You may have recognised that your child has some strong resilience traits while others may be lacking. From your initial assessment, you will have become more aware of where they need your support. It is my hope that this book has provided you with some helpful tools that you can use in the days to come.

I want to conclude this book by acknowledging that it takes resilience to parent a child from your heart. It also takes resilience to talk to a child who isn't talking back. It takes resilience to go into their room when their door is shut. It takes resilience to say 'no' when other parents are saying 'yes'. It takes resilience to do anything significant in life, especially parenting. The weight is real.

For years I have heard parents talk to me about the intense pressure they feel when parenting isn't going to plan. Parents have spoken to me about late nights spent second-guessing themselves, the pushback from children who don't get their own way and

Celebrating Resilience

the confusion that comes from receiving varying opinions from school staff and family members. To parent really well, you have to reach inside of yourself and make the best decisions you can at the time. It is an incredibly personal journey.

If you are finding parenting a challenge, know that reaching out for support is sometimes the most resilient thing you can do. If you have friends who are going through a tough time, take some time out to be kind. Lend a listening and supportive ear if you are able. It takes resilience to walk through the discomfort of parenting, but that is exactly what we need to do: keep walking.

Remember: resilience fluctuates. Therefore, today's resilience levels can be different from tomorrow's. With effort, resilience will only get stronger. I often find that resilience grows in 'spurts' and parents find themselves saying, 'All the hard work did pay off even though it didn't seem like it at the time.'

So, keep going. You are doing better than you think.

Gratitude is contagious. If we are thankful for our children, they are more likely to be thankful for themselves.

Acknowledgements

Writing a book is much more challenging than it may appear. It involves endless hours of intense research, creating and editing. Thank you to the team who helped get this project over the finish line.

A big thank you once again to the team at Big Sky Publishing who have literally brought this book to life. From the initial concept to the final edits, you have been amazing to work with. To Di, thank you for not settling for good when excellent was within our reach. You are endlessly steady and tirelessly patient, all of which are so appreciated. I know our efforts will help so many families. As you say, 'Praise for Everyday Resilience!'

Thank you to the young people and parents who have so willingly shared their stories of resilience with me. I acknowledge that strong families (and lives) don't just build themselves but are developed each time we make decisions to be courageous, grateful, empathetic, self-aware, responsible, self-caring and contributing members of the world.

My Facebook community have followed this book's journey from start to finish, and I would like to thank every single parent who took time out of their day to be with me as a I wrote its pages. It has helped me much more than you may realise. I would also like to thank Damian for being my 'international' on-call editor. You have so kindly helped me with both 'Self-harm: Why Teens Do It and How Parents Can Help' and this book. Thank you for correcting my work at lightening speeds, and introducing me to 'Med vennlig hilsen'.

Thank you to the schools who have already so enthusiastically embraced this book. I look forward to delivering many parent nights in the upcoming months, and years. To the teachers who are requesting student journals to go with this book, I'm hoping that will be my next project!

While writing this book I have come to even more deeply believe in the protective factor of family. I want to thank my parents, Alan and Pat, for modelling resilience. Thank you to my father whose endless optimism never ceases to amaze me, and to my mother, whose practicality and common sense resonates deeply with me.

Thank you to my husband, Doc Mitchell, for facing every challenge with a steady spirit and integrity. I recently said to him, 'I want to be able to look back on every challenge and say, "We made it together." To which he replied, "Not just made it, but learnt something from it."' I couldn't imagine life without you, my dear friend.

Thank you to my boys, who are the joy of my life. If I could choose just one trait to nurture in your lives it would be courage. I want you to have courage to think independently, stand alone when necessary and share your beliefs wholeheartedly. Always let your dreams be louder than your fears, and tackle every challenge knowing that you have a supportive family behind you. I will always be your biggest (and most enthusiastic) fan.

I want to finally thank every parent who reads this book and reflects on their child's resilience. May the future be stronger because of your intentional parenting.

Everyday Resilience

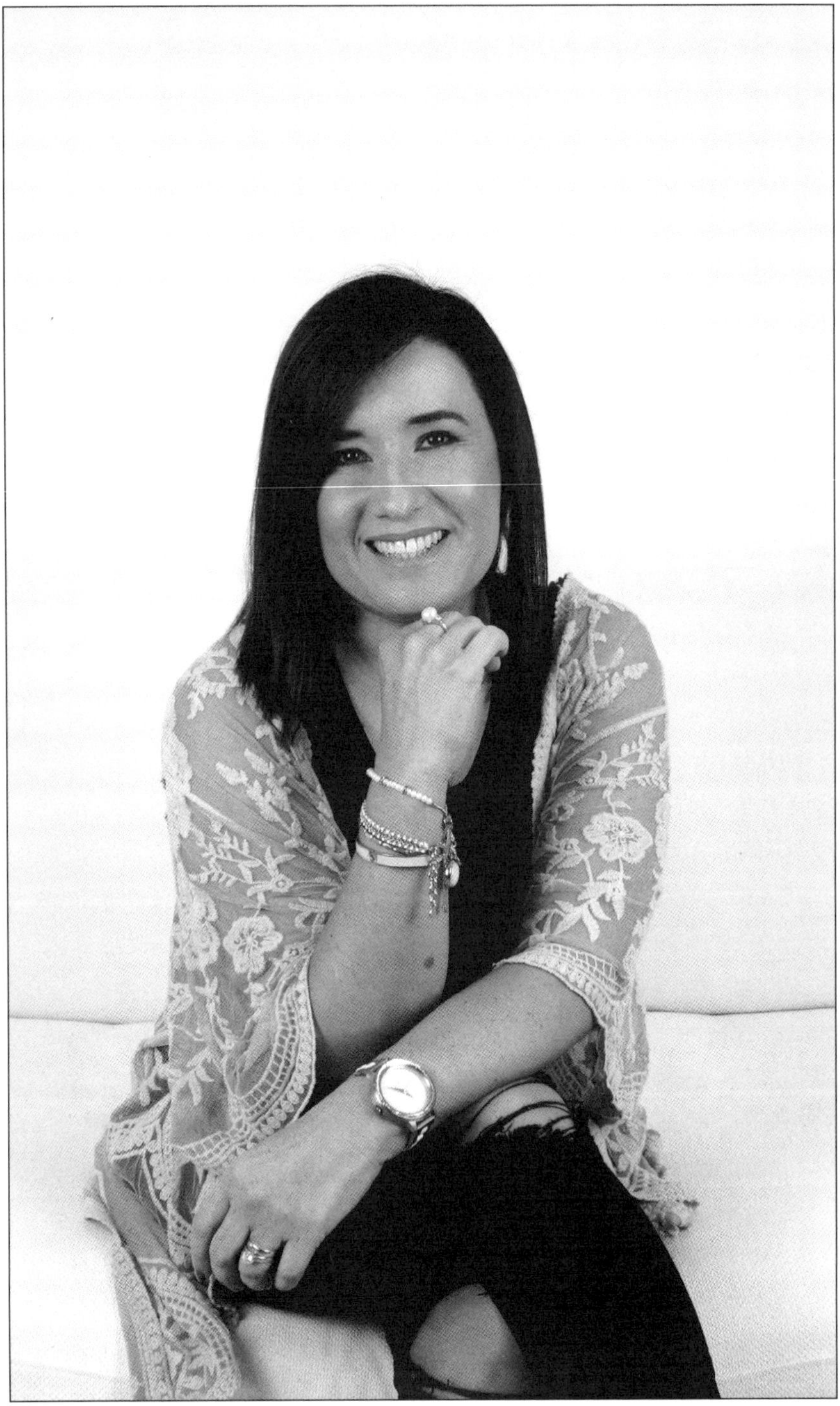

About the Author

Michelle is an award-winning speaker, author and educator whose passion is to support families.

Michelle started her career as a teacher. In 2000 Michelle left teaching and founded Youth Excel, a charity which has supported thousands of young people and their families with life skills education, mentoring and psychological services.

Michelle's hands-on experience and passion for 'all things young people' has made her a sought-after and entertaining speaker. She has a unique ability to transfer years of knowledge to a wide range of audiences.

Michelle's innovative work has been featured on the TODAY Show, Channel Ten Morning News, Today Tonight, 96fivefm, ABC radio and in countless print media including The Age, Australian Women's Weekly and the Courier Mail.

Michelle is the author of four books, and the co-author of one – *What Teenage Girls Don't Tell their Parents, Parenting Teenage Girls is the Age of a New Normal* and *Everyday Resilience: Helping Kids Handle Friendship Drama, Academic Pressure and the Self-Doubt of Growing Up*. She is the co-author of *Raising Resilient Kids*.

Michelle's books and resources have been called a 'guiding light' for parents and professionals. She has a marvellous way of speaking truth in a way that all appreciate.

She lives in Brisbane with her husband and two teenagers.

Find out more:
www.michellemitchell.org
Facebook: Michelle Mitchell – Author, Speaker, Educator
Instagram: @michellemitchellspeaker

"Michelle is a true powerhouse on this topic..."
Resilient Kids Conference

"A practical yet compassionate discussion"
Collette Smart, Psychologist and Educator

SELF HARM

WHY TEENS DO IT AND WHAT PARENTS CAN DO TO HELP

MICHELLE MITCHELL

SELF HARM

If you have a child who is struggling with self-harm, I want to remind you that you are your child's greatest advantage. What you do and how you respond matters. This book was written for you and your family — Michelle Mitchell

Self-harm is distressing and difficult for parents and caring adults to understand, as it seems to go against every instinct of self-protection and survival.

Author, educator and award-winning speaker Michelle Mitchell has over 20 years' experience working with and supporting children, parents and carers as they navigate this confronting mental health concern.

In this book she combines her experience with the latest research and interviews with experts and families to provide fresh insights into how to prevent, understand and respond to self-harm and digital self-harm.

Michelle answers questions like –

- Why does my child want to hurt themselves?
- What do I say if I suspect self-harm?
- How do I manage my child's safety?
- How do I take care of siblings and other family members?
- When should I seek support?

This unique resource will provide parents with the facts, practical help and comfort they need.

THE EVERYDAY RESILIENCE JOURNAL

A pre-teen's guide to friendships, schoolwork and growing up!

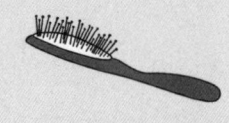

MICHELLE MITCHELL

The Everyday Resilience Journal is designed to help 8 – 12 year olds navigate friendship drama, academic pressure and the self-doubt of growing up.

Full of practical strategies, clever analogies and engaging illustrations, this journal style book makes learning about the traits of resilience fun.

The Everyday Resilience Journal guides young people through the following content:

- Handling Friendship Stuff
- Handling TOUGH Friendship Stuff
- Enjoying the Daily Routine
- Understanding Stressful Feelings
- Conquering School Work
- Knowing How to Contribute

The Everyday Resilience Journal is the perfect accompaniment to *"Everyday Resilience: Helping Kids Handle Friendship Drama, Academic Pressure and the Self-Doubt of Growing Up"*.

www.michellemitchell.org

Reference List

Ager A, 2012, "Annual Research Review: Resilience and child well-being," *Journal of Child Psychology and Psychiatry*, vol. 54, no. 4, pp. 488 - 5000.

Australian Bureau of Statistics (ABS) 2007, "National Survey of Mental Health and Wellbeing: Summary of Results". Canberra, ACT, Australia: Australian Bureau of Statistics.

Australian Bureau of Statistics, 2014,"www.abs.gov.au," (Online). Available: http://www.abs.gov.au/ausstats/abs@.nsf/Lookup/by%20Subject/3303.0~2014~Main%20Feature. [Accessed 4 Oct 2018].

Bayer J K, Ukoumunne O C, Lucas N, et al. 2011, "Risk factors for childhood mental health symptoms: National longitudinal study of Australian children", *Pediatrics* 128: e1–e15.

Bergland C, "Deconstructing the Neurobiology of Resilience," *Psychology Today*, 2016.

Bouhaddani S, v. Domburg L, Schaefer B, Doreleijers T A and Veling W, 2018,"Peer status in relation to psychotic experiences and psychosocial problems is adolescents," *Eur Child Adolsc Psychiatry*, vol. 27, pp. 701 - 710.

Bradley-Geist J C and Olson-Buchanan J B, 2014,"Helicopter Parents: An examination of the correlates of over-parenting of college students," *Education and Training*, vol. 56, pp. 314 – 328.

Branscombe J J, 2015, "Having a lot of a good thing: multiple important group memberships as a source of self-esteem," *PLOS One*, vol. 10, no. 1371, pp. 1 - 29.

Brooks R and Goldstein S, 2004, "The Power of Resilience", United States: Mc Graw-Hill Education.

Brown B, 2018, "Braving the Wilderness", London : Ebury Publishing.

Bynion T, Blumenthal H, Bilsky S, Cloutier R M and Leen-Feldner E W, 2017 "Dimensions of parenting among mothers and fathers in relation to social anxiety among female adolescents," *The Journal of Adolescents*, vol.60, pp. 11 – 15.

Reference List

Crash Course Psychology "Crash Course - Sympathic Nervous System #14," [Online]. Available: https://www.youtube.com/watch?v=0IDgBlCHVsA. [Accessed 4 October 2018].

Crash Course Psychology, "Crash Course - Emotion, Stress and Health #26," [Online]. Available: https://www.youtube.com/watch?v=4KbSRXP0wik. [Accessed 4 October 2018].

Curry O S, 2018, "A range of kindness activities boost happiness," *The Journal of Social Psychology*.

Dent M, 2016, "Real Kids in an Unreal World," Pennington Publications.

DeVore E R and Ginsburg K R. 2005, "The protective effects of good parenting on adolescents," *Curr Opin Pedatri*, vol. 17, pp. 460 - 465.

Ehrenreich S E and Underwood M K, 2017, "Bullying May Be Fueled by the Desperate Need to Belong," *Theory into Practise*, vol. 53, no. 4, pp. 265 - 270.

Emmons R A, 2007, "Thanks!: How the New Science of Gratitude Can Make You Happier", Boston: Houghton Mifflin Books

Ferguson C, Barr H and Figueroa G, 2015, "Digital poison? Three studies examining violent video games on youth," *Elsevier: Computers in Human Behaviour*, vol. 50, pp. 339 - 410.

Goethem A J V, Hoof A V, Aken M A V,. Castro B O D and Raaijmakers Q A, 2014, "Socialising adolescent volunteering: How important are parents and friends?," *Journal of Applied Developmental Psychology*, vol. 35, pp. 94 - 101.

Goldstein S and Brooks R, 2012, "Translating resilience theory for application with children and adolescents by parents, teachers, and mental health professionals," *Springer Link*, pp. 73 - 90.

Goldstein S, 2012, " Resilience in Children, Adolescents and Adults", *Springer Link*.

Gorrese A and Ruggieri R, 2013, "Peer attachment and self-esteem - A meta-analytic review," *Elsevier: Personality and Individual Differences*, vol. 55, pp. 559 - 568.

Guy S, Furber G, Leach M and Segal L, 2016, "How many children in Australia are at risk of adult mental illness?" *Australian and New Zealand Journal of Psychiatry*.

Vossen H G and Valkenburg P M, "Do social media foster or curtail adolscent empathy?," *Elsevier: Computers in Human Behaviour*, vol. 63, pp. 118 - 124, 2016.

Hall K, 2014, "Create a Sense of Belonging," [Online]. Available: https://www.psychologytoday.com/au/blog/pieces-mind/201403/create-sense-belonging. [Accessed 2018].

Humbour V K,. Zimmer-Gemback M J, Clear S and Avdagic S R E, 2018, "Emotional regulation and mindfulness in adolescents: conceptual and empirical connection and association with social anxiety symptoms," *Elsevier - Personality and Individual Differences,* vol. 134, pp. 7 - 12.

Hunter R, Grey J D and Ewen B S M, 2018, "The Nuroscience of Resilience," *Journal of the Society for Social Work and Reserach ,* vol. 9, no. 2, pp. 2334 - 3215.

Janssen I and Leblanc A G, 2010, "Systematic Review of the health benefits of phsycial activity and fitness in school-aged children and youth," *Int J Behaviour Nutr Phys Act,* vol. 7, p. 40.

Jarvis C, Interviewee, 2014, "Daring Greatly to Unlock Your Creativity with Brene Brown " [Interview]. 11 April 2014.

Jetten J, Branscombe N R, Haslam S A, Haslam C, Cruwys T, Jones J M, Cui L, Dingle G, . Liu J, Murphy S, Thai A, Walter Z, Zhang A, 2015,"Having a Lot of Good Thing: Multiple Important Group Memberships as a Source of Self-Esteem," *PLOS ONE,* vol. 10, pp. 1371,

Knapp A S, Bludmenthal H, Mischel E R, Badour C L and Leen-Feldner E W, 2016"Anxiety Sensitivity and Its factors in Relation to Generalised Anxiety Disorder among Adolescents," *J Abnorm Child Psychol,* vol. 44, pp.233 – 244.

Lawrence D, 2016 "Key findings from the second Australian Child and Adolescent Survey of Mental Health and Wellbeing," *Australian and New Zealand Journal of Psychiatry ,* vol. 50, no. 9, pp. 876 - 886.

Lawrence D, Johnson S, Hafekost J, Boterhoven de Haan K, Sawyer M, Ainley J and Zubrick S R, 2015, "The Mental Health of Children and Adolescents: Report on the Second Australian Child and Adolescent Survey of Mental Health and Wellbeing", *Paper-based publications.*

Locke J Y, 2015, "The Bonsai Child", Kelvin Grove, Queensland : Judith Locke.

Lundgaard P, 2018, "Developing Resilience in Children and Young People", New York : Routledge.

Machado Y, 2015,"Morphofunctional changes in the brain during adolescence and their impact on social interactions," *Journal of the Neurological Sciences,* vol. 357, p. 204.

Machin T M and Jeffries C H, 2017, "Threat and Opportunity: The impact of social inclusion and likeability on anonymous feedback, self-esteem and belonging," *Science Direct ,* vol. 115, pp. 1 - 6.

Masten A S and Monn A R, "Child and family resilience: a call for integrated science, practise and professional training," *Family Relations,* vol. 64, pp. 5 – 21, 2015.

Reference List

Masten A S, 2014,"Global perspectives on resilience in children and youth," Child Development, vol. 85, pp. 6 – 20.

McDowell C, MacDonncha C and Herring M, 2017 "Brief Report: Associations of physical activity with anxiety and depression symptoms and status amongst adolesecents," *Journal of Adolescence*, vol. 55, pp. 1- 4.

McMahon E M, Corcoran P and O'Regan G, 2017, "Physical activity in European adolescents and associations with anxiety, depression and well- being," *Eur Child Adolesc Psychiatry*, vol. 26, pp. 111- 112 .

Meyer F, 2016, "The Human Need for Belonging," Tedx Talks.

Miklikowski M, Duriez B, Soenens B, 2011 "Family Roots in Empathetic Related Characteristics," *Developmental Psychology*, vol. 47, no. 5, p. 1342.

Mission Australia 2017, "Youth mental health report - Youth Survey 2012 - 2016," Mission Australia and Black Dog Institute, Sydney

Mitchell M, 2008, "Parenting Teenage Girls is the Age of a New Normal," Arc House.

Noorden T H, 2015, "Empathy and involvement in bullying in children and adolscents: a systematic Review," *J Youth Adolescence,* vol. 44, pp. 637 - 657.

Online Etymology Dictionary, 2018, "Online Etymology Dictionary," [Online]. Available: https://www.etymonline.com/word/resilience. [Accessed 4 October 2018].

Padilla-Walker L M, Neilson M G and Day R D, 2015, "The role of parent warmth and hostility on adolescents' prosocial behaviour towards multiple targets," *American Psychological Association,* vol. 30, no. 3, pp. 331 - 340.

Pillow D R, Malone G P and Hale W J,2014, "The need to belong and its association with fully satisfying relationships: A tale of two measures," *Elsevier,* vol. 0191, pp. 259 - 264.

Praszkier R, 2014,"Empathy, mirror neurons and SYNC," *Mind and Society*, vol. 15, pp. 1 – 25.

Ringesisen T and Raufelder D, 2015,"The interplay of parent support, parental pressure and test anxiety – Gender differences in adolescents," *Journal of Adolescents,* vol.45, pp 67 – 79.

Rizzolati G and Destro M, 2008, "Mirror Neurons," *Scholarpedia*, vol.1, pp. 2055.

Rowland L and Curry O S, 2018, "A range of kindness activities boost happiness," *The Journal of Social Psychology*, pp. 1940 – 1183.

Russo S J, Murrough J W, Hu Han M, Charney D S and Nestler E J, 2012, "Neurobiology of Resilience," *Nat Nuerosci.*, vol. 15, pp. 1475 - 1484.

Ruvalcaba N A, Gallegos J, Borges A and Gonzalez N, 2017, "Extracurriculum activites and group belonging as a protective facts in adolescents," *Science Direct*, vol. 23, no. 1, pp. 45 - 51.

Schleider J and Weisz J, 2016, "Reducing risk for anxiety and depression in adolescents: effects of a single session intervention teaching that personality can change," *Behaviour and Research Therapy*, vol. 87, pp. 170 - 181.

Silk C, 2018, "Factors influencing the development of empathy and pro-social behaviour amongst adolescents: a systematic review," Children and Youth Services Review.

Smith R, 2015, "Adolescents emotional engagement in friends' problems and joys: Association of empathic distress and empathetic joy with friendship quality, depression and anxiety," *Journal of Adolescents*, vol. 45, pp. 103 - 111.

Sonnentag T L and Barnett M A, 2015, "Role of Moral Identity and Moral Courage Characteristics in Adolescents' Tendencies to be a Moral Rebel," *Ethics and Behaviour*, vol. 26, no. 4, pp. 277 - 299.

Spaulding S, 2013 "Mirror Neurons and Social Cognition," *Mind and Language*, vol.28, pp. 233 – 257.

Takeuchi M S, Miyaoka H, Tomoda A, Suzuki M, Liu Q and Kitamura T, "The effect of interpersonal touch during childhood on adult attachment and depression: a neglected area of family and developmental psychology?", *Journal of Child and Family Studies*, vol. 19, pp. 109 – 117, 2010.

Underwood M K and Ehrenreich S E, 2014,"Bullying may be fuelled by the desperate need to belong," *Theory into Practise*, pp. 1543 – 0421.

Van Noorden T H J, Haselager G L T, Cillessen A H N and Bukowski W N, 2015,"Empathy and Involvement in Bullying in Children and Adolescents: A Systematic Review," *J Youth Adolescence*, vol. 44. Pp. 637 – 657.

Vignoli E, 2015. "Career indecision and career exploration amonst older frendsh adolescents: the specific role that gender trait anxiety and future school and career anxiety," *Journal of Vocational Behaviour*, vol. 89, pp. 182 - 191.

View sample pages, reviews and more information on this and other titles at **www.bigskypublishing.com.au**

Reference List

Warner E, 1993,"Risk, Resilience and Recovery: Perspectives from the Kauai Longitudinal Study," *Developmental and Psychopathology,* vol. 04, no. 5, p. 503.

World Health Organisation, 2010 "Global Recommendations for Physical Activity of Health," Geneva.

Zautra A J, 2010, "Resilience: Promoting Well-being Through Recovery, Sustainability and Growth," *Research in Human Development* , vol. 7, no. 3, pp. 221 - 238.